IT'S MY TURN

TO BE AN ENTREPRENEUR

Everything you need to know <u>BEFORE</u> you start a business

---

Frank E. Bisconti
CEO and Founder
Consultus Management Partners, LLC

CONSULTUS PUBLISHING
West Dundee, Illinois

The information contained in this book should not be viewed or considered as a substitute for competent legal, accounting, tax or business advice.

Copyright © 2011 by Frank E Bisconti
ISBN-13: 978-1463766016

First Consultus Publishing Paperback Edition 2011

All rights reserved. No part of this book may be used or reproduced in any manner whatsoever without the expressed written permission of Frank E Bisconti.

CONSULTUS PUBLISHING

Consultus Publishing
a division of Consultus Management Partners, LLC
34W874 Avenue Chapelle, Suite 500
West Dundee, IL 60118

www.consultusmp.com
Send book comments to: **info@consultusmp.com**

Inquiries regarding consulting services by Frank Bisconti can be directed to:

Frank E Bisconti, CEO
Consultus Management Partners, LLC
34W874 Avenue Chapelle, Suite 500
West Dundee, IL 60118

fbisconti@consultusmp.com
Office: 224.356.6600

Dedication

This book is dedicated to my brilliant and talented wife, Lynette, the president of The Gateway for Cancer Research, who has been my inspiration and the motivation behind all of my business successes and whose incredible patience and understanding has made this book possible.

And to Frankie, my 13 year old son, whom I hope achieves his dream of someday owning the world's largest home at over 3 million square feet. All I can say is that is a lot of furniture. May the economy be with you!

CONSULTUS PUBLISHING

CONTENTS

About the Author 7

Introduction 9

1 Are You Sure You want to be an Entrepreneur? 14

2 The Truth About Unemployment 21

3 Should I Start a Business During a Recession? 29

4 What to do BEFORE you Start a Business 46

5 The Art (and Science) of the Business Plan 63

6 Finding Capital to Start a Business 69

7 Red Flags About Business Partners 85

8 Managing Money – Cash Is King 115

9 Sales – Lifeblood of Your Business 126

10 Marketing – Success Depends on It 132

11 Building Your Team 155

12 A Little Technology Goes a Long Way 163

13 Exit Strategies 168

Appendices
- Personal Strengths and Weaknesses
  Evaluation Form — *178*
- Start-Up Costs Worksheet — *181*
- Business Selection Worksheet — *182*
- Business Analysis Worksheet — *185*
- 2010 Accounting Software Review
  Product Comparisons — *187*
- Sample Business Plan — *188*
-Sample Marketing Plan — *192*

Glossary of Business Terms
201

About the Author

Frank Bisconti is the founder and Chief Executive Officer of Consultus Management Partners, LLC, a successful, Chicago-based business consulting firm that specializes in corporate turnarounds, reorganizations and assisting new and emerging companies build sound, functional infrastructures to help achieve success.

Prior to launching Consultus in 2007, Frank worked for three (3) public companies and five (5) private companies in executive level positions. Frank began working at age 15 in his father's McDonald's Restaurants. After graduating from Seton Hall University in 1978, he continued working with his father as Vice President and Controller handling the restaurants' accounting and reporting requirements, inventory control, community relations and advertising. At the same time, Frank was also in the entertainment business performing as a singer until 1988; as well as starting and managing Top Billing Records, Prime Time Entertainment, an entertainment production company and Top Talent, Inc., a theatrical booking agency.

In 1987, Frank joined the executive team at Home Shopping Network, Inc. shortly after it had gone public. During his 7 years at HSN, he held positions of Director, Business Analysis; Director, Subsidiary Operations; and Division President of HSN Travel, Inc. Frank was also a member of HSN's Executive Strategic Planning Committee.

In 1996, Frank went on to become Chief Financial Officer of a national packaging and distribution company. The company doubled its sales and quadrupled its profits during his five (5) years. A new opportunity allowed Frank to become Chief Operating Officer and Chief Financial Officer of a national brand marketing and promotional products company that quickly became a Top 50 Distributor. Sales jumped a whopping 400% during his four (4) years by building a great human capital team, sound operations, and a solid sales and marketing strategy.

Now, an author, Frank is expanding his interests to include a radio talk show launching in August 2011. Keep an eye out for new projects and books as he leverages his business experiences to build his own American Dream of being a successful entrepreneur.

Introduction

The world is a changing place. The United States has just gone through its most severe recession in over 30 years. Many people have lost their jobs and the reality is that a great many of them will not get those same jobs back. America's business models are changing driven by innovation, technology and as little labor as possible.

So what do you do when you get caught up in a corporate downsizing? What if the prospects of returning to that same job are extremely poor? Do you have the skills to transition to another field of work quickly to continue to support yourself and your family? Or is it time to start controlling your own destiny and start a business of your own? Are you ready to be an entrepreneur?

On the face, that simple question sounds like a rally cry for the unemployed to go out and start a business. It is not. Starting a business does indeed require passion and drive, and being out of work, having no income and a family to take care of can be incredible motivators to get into that anger-driven mindset of, "I'll just do it myself." But that very simple question, "Are you ready to be an entrepreneur?" is far more than a rally cry.

You may have the motivation, but motivation does not start or run a successful business. To be "ready" requires you to answer a few other questions as well, such as:

- Are you prepared to work 80 hours a week when you are used to working 40?
- Do you have a product or service you KNOW (not think) you can sell?
- Do you have enough money to start and run a company for one year?
- Do you know how to manage money? People? Customers? Technology?
- What do you really know about marketing?
- Do you have a plan to start, run and even sell your business?
- Managing success is easy, but do you know how to manage failure?

Being an entrepreneur can be exciting, answering to yourself and not an incompetent boss. Earning more money is a great prospect for you, your family and your future. Running your own business controls your income and your employment. There is the opportunity to become part of the American Dream and become wealthy, to be respected, to be a business leader in your community, to help others.

So why doesn't everyone take the big step and become an entrepreneur? Ah, because there are also risks that go along with the potential rewards.

Lesson #1 in business: **MAXIMIZE YOUR STRENGTHS AND MINIMIZE YOUR WEAKNESSES**. But in order to do this, you must first know all of your strengths and weaknesses. Do you?

Let's find out if you are really ready to become an entrepreneur, and if you are, read on and learn the basics of starting and running a business successfully. Learn from others' mistakes, do what works and avoid what does not work. Determine if, in fact, you are truly prepared to say, *"It's My Turn to be an Entrepreneur."*

IT'S MY TURN

TO BE AN ENTREPRENEUR

Everything you need to know
<u>BEFORE</u> you start a business

Chapter 1

Are You Sure You Want to be an Entrepreneur?

If your 18 year old son came to you and said, "Mom and Dad, I think I'm going to get married next month" you know how you would feel and you would want to talk to him about all of the pros and cons of being married, especially at such a young age. You would want to impart your wisdom and experience and to make sure that he is going to make an informed decision. And the likelihood is that you will probably strongly object to his marriage plan, possibly admiring his love and passion for his wife-to-be, but also criticizing him for a lack of experience in managing relationships, money, occupations, future goals and a litany of other things.

Well, starting a new business is a lot like getting married. You will hear from friends and relatives all of the criticisms that you would most likely share with your son. You will be called crazy, that the chances of success are poor, you don't have enough money to start and run a business, you have no experience, you will hear about the benefits and security associated with a steady job, and the fear and concern about stepping out of America's mainstream occupational behavior. Effectively, all of the same criticisms, just in a different form, that you will share with your 18 year old son who wants to get married.

So, let's examine if becoming an entrepreneur is truly what you want to do and that it is not something that just sounds like a good idea or worse, something that you think you should do because you feel you are running out of options not being employed. Let's also take a look at your own personal strengths and weaknesses and see if you are suited to starting and running a business.

First, go through the relatively simple, but insightful process of evaluating your current situation. This can be done by evaluating your personal strengths and weaknesses. Consider where you and your family are now. This process should also include both tangible and intangible elements.

Following are 12 points to evaluate BEFORE investing your first dollar into a new business. Answer them truthfully. You may be surprised at what you learn about yourself. It will provide you with great insight into whether or not you should be considering becoming an entrepreneur at this time in your life:

1. What is your current financial situation? How much money do you have saved, how much steady income do you have, what are your monthly expenses?

2. How are your family relationships? Starting a new business will certainly change the family dynamics. Can everyone deal with a major change?

3. If you are currently employed, do you have the time to dedicate to a new business?

4.   What is your current quality of life? This is important to evaluate because starting a new business involves a great deal of change and stress, long hours of work, challenges. If your current quality of life is poor, you will simply be adding to your problems and may make decisions based on frustrating family or work related elements of your life and not on the business. For some, this may be a motivator, for others a recipe for disaster. You need to honestly evaluate your current circumstances.

5. Make a list of things that make you happy and unhappy. You may be surprised and see a recurring theme develop relative to what you are truly passionate about. This might help to guide you into what kind of business you should consider.

6. Define your ideal life. There are no right answers. The sky should be the limit. How much income would you like to make? How big of a business would you like to run? Do you want to retire at a certain age? Do you want to live somewhere else? Do you want to do charity work? Do you want to develop new skills or talents? Anything goes.

7. List your skills and capabilities. With a goal of achieving your ideal life, what skills, experiences and strengths do you have to help you to achieve that ideal life? Hint: your skills should not be only professional, but life skills as well. In the back of this book is a *Personal Strengths and Weaknesses Worksheet*. Complete it, but you must be honest.

8. List your personal and professional accomplishments. If you have been successful at certain things in the past, you may be able to leverage those experiences when starting a new business. Remember, maximize your strengths.

9. Try to define your perfect work style. This will help to determine the kind of business that best suits you. For example, do you like to work on your own or manage a team of people? Would those people be white collar or blue collar workers? Do you like to travel, work from home, in an office, a manufacturing environment, or a retail business? Do you envision your new company selling a service or a product? Would that service or product be sold to businesses or directly to consumers? Are you looking to minimize risk in return for lesser but steady rewards or are you willing to take on more risk for greater rewards?

10. Try to create a Personal Mission Statement. Define yourself, your goals, principles and priorities into a document that is one page or less. Elements of a mission statement could include why you want to work, who benefits from your business, the kind of people with whom you would like to interact, and the purpose of your business.

11. Define your ideal business. What kind of business would make you happy? Passionate? Driven to succeed? Personally and professionally satisfying? Hint: You can define more than one. It is always good to have options to consider.

12. Define your long term strategy. The type of business you start and run may be influenced by your long term strategy. For how many years do you want to run this business? Are you planning to pass it along to your children? Would they even want it? Do you want to build it up, sell it, and then retire? Answering these questions will help to determine how the business (and the money) is managed.

If you have found this first exercise to be boring and tedious, a waste of your time, and seemingly with no purpose relative to starting a new business you have successfully answered the question, *"Are you sure you want to be an entrepreneur?"* You do not. Put the book down and continue looking for a job.

As discussed in the Introduction, passion and dedication to start and run a business is important, but that and a dollar will get you a cup of coffee. Running a business is a process and knowing all of the elements of a business will, in turn, ensure success. If you are to be the Chief Executive Officer (CEO) you need to know about yourself first and what is most important to you and your family. Starting a business that you will hate will certainly end in disaster, especially if you have to work 80 hours a week to make it successful. Remember that job you hated, how hard you worked, and for what? You don't want to repeat mistakes. Minimize your risks. This will be a recurring theme throughout this book.

Conversely, if you have gone through this exercise and feel you have effectively and honestly evaluated your circumstances, your life, your family, your strengths and weaknesses, your passions, and your goals read on. You just may be ready to become an entrepreneur.

Chapter 2

The Truth about Unemployment

Calculating Unemployment

The unemployment rate is considered by most economists to be one of the most important measures of economic health. Economists believe the greater proportion of people that are not working, the worse the economy is likely to be performing.

The basic calculation used to find the unemployment rate is the total amount of people who are out of work but seeking employment, divided by the total amount of people in the labor force. This seems like a simple calculation, but there are some caveats. The "labor force" is defined as anyone who is either currently working at a job, or actively seeking a job." People that do not have jobs and are not actively seeking to get one are not considered part of the labor force, and therefore, are not technically unemployed. One "unofficial" barometer is "seeking a job within the past month is used as qualification for being considered in the labor force."

Collecting Data

Calculating the unemployment rate relies heavily upon collecting data about the work force. While the calculation of unemployment in and of itself is simple, getting correct numbers for the total amount of people in the labor force--and the total amount of people looking for jobs--requires constant surveying. Every month, the Bureau of Labor Statistics conducts a survey of households, known as the Current Population Survey, which is used as a sample for the overall population. It would be impractical to survey every household and keep track of every unemployed person each month. Sufficiently large sample groups are used to make statistically accurate approximations for the size of the labor force and those without jobs.

Shortcomings of Unemployment Data

The unemployment rate is a useful calculation, but it has several shortcomings. Since a worker must be actively looking for employment to be considered in the labor force and counted as unemployed, workers that are discouraged and not actively seeking a job because there are none to be had are not counted as unemployed, even if they would want to work if jobs were available. There are also a large amount of workers that do not work at traditional jobs, such as contractor and freelancers who may be considered employed if they are doing work occasionally, but the amount of work they are doing may be far less than a traditionally employed worker.

How is the Unemployment Rate Actually Calculated Each Month?

Surveyors from the Bureau of Labor Statistics (BLS) visit 60,000 households every month and ask a number of questions to determine each person's employment status. If someone works full-time, part-time, or is self-employed, they are considered employed. If someone does not have a job of any kind, but has been looking for one for the past four weeks, they are considered unemployed. If someone does not have a job and isn't looking for one, they are considered outside of the labor force.

The rate is then calculated as the number of people who are "actively seeking jobs" (the government's definition of "unemployed") divided by the number of people who have jobs plus those people "actively looking" (the government's definition of the "labor force"). If you are not actively looking for work but are also unemployed, you are not considered part of the calculation.

Let's use an example to better understand the point and how the official unemployment rate is highly skewed and misleading.

Example: The Bureau of Labor Statistics conducts a survey of 60,000 U.S. households with 120,000 respondents. The survey findings are:

- 75,000 people have full time jobs either working for an employer, are self-employed or own their own business;

- 10,000 report they are actively seeking work;

- The remaining 35,000 are not considered part of the labor force. Some report they are in school, disabled or unable to work; however, even if all 35,000 reported they were available and able but simply not seeking employment they would not be part of the calculation.

In the example above, the unemployment rate would be 11.8%. If the 35,000 people not employed were included in the calculation, the unemployment rate would be a staggering 37.5%!!

Problems with Misleading Information

1. Americans believe the unemployment rate to be about 9.5% based on information reported as on June 30, 2011. If ALL truly unemployed Americans were reported in the calculation, economists estimate that the real effective unemployment rate in the U.S. could be as high as 20%;

2. The BLS uses a sample size of 60,000 households to represent the 120 million or so that actually exist in the U.S. It is very difficult to determine how well the total population is represented by the 60,000 households randomly selected. Many factors drive unemployment. If

any or all of these determinants are overstated or understated the unemployment rate can be grossly misrepresented or biased;

3. People that are technically employed but that do not earn a true liveable income also skew the results. For example, a self-employed man running a small company may be the president and be employed, but circumstances only allow him to draw $500 per month out of his business to support his family. He is considered employed. Part time workers, farmers, seasonal workers, certain construction jobs, tourist companies all exclude those employees in the unemployed calculation;

4. The survey double or triple counts people that have multiple jobs, for example, if you work part time at McDonald's, sell Mary Kay cosmetics, and mow lawns to make extra money you may be counted as having three (3) jobs;

5. Students are normally excluded from the calculation; however, if a student decides to look for a job he becomes part of the official "labor force" until he finds one or stops looking for one. Also, if someone is laid off or fired from a job

and they are finishing their last week at work and the survey includes their household, that person would be counted as employed, even though he will be unemployed at the end of the week;

6. Others are classified as employed as long as they "technically" still have a job. If someone is on a leave of absence, on a temporary layoff (even though it might become permanent), or on disability with no intention to return to work they are all considered employed.

So who should be count to determine the true unemployment rate?

Should we count someone as unemployed if they want a job but is not actively seeking one? Should someone who simply doesn't feel like working be classified as unemployed or out of the labor force entirely? Should disabled citizens who cannot work be classified as unemployed? Should self-employed people with little or no income be classified as unemployed? Should students be included in the calculation at all?

The Bottom Line

You can now better understand how the U.S. unemployment rate can be misleading. Prior to 2009, the U.S. unemployment rate hovered around 4.5% for many years. It became a benchmark for measuring the strength of the country's employment status, and consequently, its health. Now, the rate has been at or about 9.2% for the past several years and defined as America's "new normal." From this chapter, we now know the true unemployment rate is not anywhere near 9.2% but probably closer to 18%. The most important "takeaway" is that the "new normal rate" of 9.2% is a marketing ploy by the Federal government to acclimate people to the fact that the unemployment rate will not be decreasing any time soon, that this economy is how it is going to be for quite some time.

If you are planning to return to work soon, do not manage your future on that assumption. It is more likely you will not. It is time to consider alternative plans on how to manage your career and your future. It is time to consider becoming your own boss and controlling your own future. But are you ready for such a big change?

Chapter 3

Should I Start a Business During a Recession?

A quick study of American history relative to economic slowdowns and recessions shows us that most recessions since World War II last about 10 months, followed by a cycle of growth and prosperity that averages 50 months. So, if the U.S. is in a recession or economic slowdown, does it make sense to start a business now or wait until the economy "turns around?"

The pessimist will advise that if things are bad now, why incur risk by spending money to start a business without really knowing when the slowdown will end? The optimist will counter with a response that suggests that based on history, we do know when the slowdown will end (on average) and that by starting a business during a recession allows you to be ready to take advantage of the economic upturn when it hits. You will find that most people will have their own list of why NOT to start a business; therefore, by starting a business now you will have less competition. Let the others wait to begin pursing their dreams.

Philosophy aside, there are many good reasons to start a business during a recession.

1. There is less competition. During a recession, you see many small businesses close, which creates an unrealistic fear that opening a new business may result in the same outcome. There are many reasons why businesses fail in a recession, and most have to do with poor management and not the economy itself. Planning is not a strong suit of small businesses. Knowing how to plan for future business challenges ensures the longevity of the business. So, if most are going to wait, there will necessarily be less competition relative to new business start-ups. If there is less competition, there will be greater access to all of the things you need to start a business.

2. Investors have more money to invest. With less start-up competition and existing businesses in protection mode and not expanding, there are greater opportunities to find start-up capital. During a recession investors become more reluctant to invest in the stock market or real estate because these traditional investment vehicles usually slide downward with the recession. Family, friends, private investors and even banks become more receptive to investing into new business opportunities that have a sound business plan. Also, you can take advantage of having trusted relationships with family and friends who may feel more secure investing money with a known entity.

3. Assets you need to start a business cost less. Traditionally, during a recession businesses buy less office furniture, computers, phone systems, inventory, equipment and office space as they try to hold onto their cash. Economics 101 tells us that, in general, if the demand goes down and inventory goes up, then costs will go down. Starting a business requires an investment into certain assets that have a cost. If you can buy what you need for less money now, you will have lower start-up costs for your new business. For example, if you are looking to start a retail business, as commercial real estate landlords see businesses closing and defaulting on their leases, this becomes an opportunity to go in and lease premium space at discounted pricing. The same is true for warehouse space and all of the other tangible assets you might need to start your new business.

4. Labor is less expensive. As many lose their jobs during a recession, the number of available workers increases creating greater competition for jobs. Again, the laws of supply and demand will show us that if there are more people looking for jobs than the number of jobs available, the employers can offer lower wages because there is so much competition. In my own personal experience while job searching during a recession, I have encountered situations where as many as 500 candidates applied for the same position; and several times I was not hired in favor of someone less qualified but willing to work for less money.

5. Labor is more motivated to perform well. In a challenging job market, the prospect of becoming employed is very exciting for potential candidates, more so than when there are more jobs and less candidates when the candidates feel more comfortable demanding higher wages and benefits. During a recession, when you interview candidates for any level job, knowing that there is a large pool of candidates from which to select, you, as the employer, can be demanding and patient, looking for the best candidates who are enthusiastic, motivated and truly desirous of wanting to work for your company. In the long run, these characteristics will benefit your business by having employees who are truly dedicated to you, the company and your customers.

6. Labor is more qualified. With more candidates competing for the same job, you will have the opportunity to find and hire better-qualified people. People with years of experience, say at a Director's level, may be willing to take a step back and work as a Manager just so he or she can get back to work. This gives you and your business a chance to hire more talented people, people to whom you might normally not have access.

7. Companies become more receptive to changing suppliers. If you are considering a business that sells a product or service to other businesses, you may have a real opportunity to secure new business very quickly. In a recession, existing businesses look to reduce costs. Starting a new business with much lower overhead than your larger competitors may give you a significant competitive advantage by being able to offer your products or services at lower prices to prospective clients. If you are unable to offer lower pricing because of economies of scale, you may still have an advantage by offering greater value, personal attention, faster response times when resolving problems, easier access, etc. Larger businesses understand that a lower cost does not necessarily translate to a better value. Regardless, during a recession you will have a greater opportunity to present your product or service to prospective clients because they are looking to save money or improve productivity.

8. Better credit becomes available from suppliers. As inventories rise or fewer services are contracted, businesses become more flexible with their pricing terms and credit offerings. If your new business needs to purchase inventory, for example, you may be able to negotiate 45 or even 60 day payment terms versus the more traditional 30 day terms when times are good and demand is high. Longer payment terms give you greater control of your cash, and as you will read later on, cash is king. The longer you can hold onto your cash the more stable your business will be.

9. There may be public relations advantages. Starting a business during a recession seems contrary to common trends, therefore, there may be an opportunity to secure public relations or media coverage for your new business because you are "bucking the trend." The media loves creative thinkers and those that appear to be doing something different. It is noteworthy, therefore, by presenting an alternative view to starting and running a business during a recession may make for an interesting story. There is nothing like free advertising to drive new clients to your new business.

Remember, the world does not stop when there is a recession, it just changes. If you know how to take advantage of the temporarily changed economic environment, you can prosper. People and businesses continue to buy goods and services, just under different conditions. Provide the right product or service at the right price and your new business will generate sales even in a recession.

If you manage your new business properly by having a sound business model and you control your costs, you can still be successful. Small businesses have certain advantages, for example, they can change strategies or cut costs much more quickly than a larger company. You can hire more experienced employees that may be laid off by larger firms.

So, if you are going to launch a new business during a recession, here are some recommendations on how to go about deciding on what type of business, in general, might work best during these times:

1. Sell a necessity-based product or service. What this means is there are certain goods or services that people or businesses need to buy regardless of the economy. Examples of such products are food, computers, clothing, and maintenance services. Avoid selling things that require discretionary spending like luxury items and designer clothing where people can wait to make purchases.

2. Consider buying an existing business as opposed to starting one from scratch. Although you may pay more when buying an existing business, what you do buy is name recognition and brand identity, an existing client base, an income stream, and experienced, trained employees. It is easier to build on an existing income stream than to start one from nothing.

3. Minimize your full-time staff. By keeping your full-time staff at a minimum, you will spend less money on labor, benefits and taxes. No one said that running your own business was going to be easy, so you may have to do more of the work yourself. Use part-time employees or contract labor, even consider outsourcing certain jobs if this makes sense. Keep your labor costs under control. Labor tends to be one of the most expensive line items in running most businesses.

4. Control your costs. One distinct advantage of running your own business is that you decide how your money is spent. During economic slowdowns, control your costs! Develop an operating plan and a budget and make sure you are not spending more on things like office supplies, advertising, travel and entertainment, legal and accounting fees, etc. If sales decrease respond quickly by reducing costs to maintain your bottom line (your profits.)

5. When selling to businesses don't be afraid to discount your products or services to secure a few major clients. Cash flow, which will be discussed in Chapter 7, is primary to running and maintaining a successful business. Determine how much revenue you need to cover your expenses each month and do whatever you need to do to ensure you have enough money coming into your company to cover these costs. This translates to positive cash flow which means that you will not have to put money out of your own pocket (or borrow money) in order to keep your business running. Discount what you offer to secure a few larger clients that will keep the money flowing. Worry about profit later.

Now that we have discussed whether or not it makes sense to start a business during a recession, what if you decide to go ahead and do it? Selecting the right business certainly improves your chances of success. Having product knowledge or industry experience allows you to make fewer mistakes because you will deal with a product or service with which you are familiar. You understand things like demand, pricing, profit margins, inventory requirements, and challenges associated with the selling process. There are clearly advantages to starting a business where you have some experience.

However, one element of the decision making process is for you to be passionate about your new business. Just because you have product knowledge or industry experience does not necessarily mean that you enjoy that industry. Actually, the contrary may be true. You may want to venture off into something completely new or something that you have always wanted to try but have not had the opportunity to explore.

So should you even consider starting a business with little or no industry experience? Should you seriously consider starting a business with no real business experience? The answer to both of these questions is that a lack of industry or business experience should not dissuade you from at least exploring new opportunities, especially if it is something about which you feel strongly. If you believe you are smart or adaptable, you can certainly learn the ins and outs of a new industry and there are plenty of books or people who can provide expert advice on running a business or to help you get started.

Entrepreneurs can be successful in unknown environments by heeding a few simple tips:

1. Start a company that provides a market solution. Avoid a pet idea or something so unique where there is little or no evidence to support that it will be successful. This concept speaks directly to the law of supply and demand. Find a demand, provide a solution. This could be a product or a service. Do not try to create a market for what you may believe is a unique and novel idea that people will love. If you do have such a novel idea, find ways to test the marketplace to see if there will be a demand BEFORE you start your business. Many entrepreneurs have not followed this advice and have taken the "build it and they will come" business model. This is extremely risky and usually results in a very high failure rate.

2. Maximize your strengths, minimize your weaknesses. For example, if your work experience has been in retailing, you may have years of experience understanding customer behaviors, product demand, customer service requirements, and retail environments. You may want to move away from the specific retail experience that you have had; however, know that such experience can transcend industry lines. Having worked directly with customers could certainly be helpful if you wanted to avoid retail altogether but you want to sell a product or service directly to businesses. Conversely, if you believe you should be the next manager of the New York Yankees, you may find that your retail experience will be of little assistance.

3. Select an industry with low entry barriers. Each business type has different start-up requirements that go beyond start-up costs. If you want to start a business with which you are unfamiliar select one with as few entry barriers as possible. You may want to steer clear of businesses that require developing a large sales force, have high regulatory or product safety requirements or patents that could be challenged by competitors.

4. Seek expert advice. If you are inexperienced or do not understand an industry there are many experts that do. There are networking groups, online resources, printed materials, consultants, and even competitors where you can learn about industry nuances. Remember, one of the keys to building a successful business is to minimize your risks and your mistakes. Do not use guesswork to make important business decisions. If you don't know, find someone who does. Not only will it save you time, but it will certainly save you money in the long run by not having to undo something you may do simply because you have no direct experience in that area.

5. Do not be afraid of criticism. Although you may become your own boss and master of your domain, being humble and keeping an open mind about criticism can be beneficial. Use industry knowledgeable people for their opinions and accept their criticisms. Encourage them to analyze your ideas or strategies, shoot holes in them, and challenge you. The more information you have on which to make a decision the more likely you will make the right decision.

If you are now ready to seriously consider becoming an entrepreneur, here are a few more tips to consider:

1. A million dollar idea will not command a million dollar investment. Do not develop a business plan that requires a million dollars of venture capital to launch the business. Investors will not ever give you the money regardless of how good you may think your idea is. If you truly believe you need large sums of money to start your business, start over. Scale down your plans and build a business model that can be started on the proverbial "shoestring." Show how a nominal investment can launch a successful business, and that over time, sales and profits will grow. Make your business work. If you are able to build a profitable business, it will become much easier to secure a larger investment later on for expansion.

2. Your business is a start-up, act like it. There is nothing wrong with dreaming about building a multi-million dollar business, if that is one of your goals; however, do not act like your business generates millions of sales dollars by leasing large offices, purchasing expensive office furniture, leasing cars, and spending large sums of money entertaining prospective clients. Understand and control your costs and manage your cash flow so it is always positive, if possible.

3. Be passionate. Find a business that you will love. If you build a business around your passion, your strengths and your talents you will have a much greater chance of success than one where you 'chase a dream' of high profits in some industry about which you have little interest. If you are not passionate about what you are doing, it will show to your employees and your customers. You will be surprised how customers react to entrepreneurs that truly love the business they are in. The converse is also true. If you dislike the business you are in, people will sense this and will not want to do business with you. Love your business. It will also make you happy.

4. **Focus.** Although it can be exciting to start a new business, selecting the right business requires you to focus on one good idea. Do not get distracted with every new opportunity that may come along and think you can changes gears or worse, add new ideas to a developing business plan. Train yourself to do one thing well and build on that idea. Do not become a jack of all trades, become a master of one.

5. **The 30-second "pitch."** Be able to present your new business concept to an investor, banker, industry expert, potential customer, family or friends in 30 seconds. You should have a clear understanding of your company's mission, the product or service offering, and its goals and be able to present them in a clear and concise manner. Modify your pitch for whom you are speaking, be brief and to the point.

When starting a business, be smart. Leverage what you know and seek advice on things you do not know. Although no one likes recessions or economic slowdowns, the reality is they will eventually turn around into times of prosperity. If you want to start a business during an economic slowdown, take advantage of what the market has to offer in terms of buying necessary assets and hiring people, but manage your business to accommodate the slower sales period. Minimize your risks, run your business's finances tightly and start a business that provides a market solution. A market solution can be a service or product. Use your business experiences to your advantage and seek expert advice if you do not understand things about your new business's industry.

Chapter 4

What to Do BEFORE You Start a Business

Starting a new business is not as simple as ready, set, go. A great deal of thought and preparation must go into the process of starting a business. Before you can start selling your product or service there are many things to do to ensure that your business will run properly and that you and your assets are protected. Let's begin to identify those things that are essential to starting a new business, and the whys and wherefores of doing all of these things BEFORE the first day of making your product or service available for sale. In the Appendix section you will find a "Business Start-Up Checklist" for when the time comes for you to begin the process of launching a new, real business.

The first step in the process is almost obvious, you must select a business. There are thousands of businesses from which to select. If you do not have a clear vision, making a choice can be difficult. You want to select a business that you will love and be passionate about but also one that will be financially viable (it will make you money.)

You will need to decide if you want to buy an existing business or start a new one. Will your business sell a product or a service? Will your offering be sold to consumers or to businesses? Are you considering a traditional "brick and mortar" storefront or a web-based business? What about a franchise? What is the best type of business and what are the entry barriers for each opportunity?

For those of you that do not have a clear vision of what you would like your business to be, deciding on the right business can be a stumbling block, but as is everything else about running a business, you will need to go through a process to determine what the best business for you and your family will be. If there is not a particular business about which you feel passionate, then consider your skills and experiences. There will certainly be an advantage to running a business in which you have some knowledge and experience, but it is not necessarily a requirement. Start by defining your personal goals. For example, are you seeking a certain income level? Do you want to grow your business into a major company or do you want to keep it smaller and simpler? How much time do you want to dedicate to your company? Do you want to deal with having many employees, just a few or possibly even none at all?

Next, determine a business sector. Try to list the general business industries to which you are drawn, but also list some that you absolutely do not want to get involved in. There are hundreds of industries. Once you determined one or more industries, consider your strengths, weaknesses, skills and experiences. What types of businesses can present the best opportunities and which ones the greatest threats?

Do not become overwhelmed by the selection process. Being an entrepreneur is all about making decisions every day. This will be your first major one. If you truly struggle with making a decision on the type of business you would like to start, consider a partnership with someone more comfortable making decisions or, unfortunately, do not become an entrepreneur at all. As an entrepreneur, decision making will become your life. If this makes you uncomfortable, consider other income options.

One resource that is readily available is the North American Industrial Classification System of Businesses (NAICS). This system identifies approximately 1,200 industries each of which includes any number of specific businesses. The industries are grouped into general categories such as construction, financial, leisure and hospitality, manufacturing, professional services, wholesale and retail trades and many more. Once you have decided on the perfect business, the start-up process begins. The start-up process entails all of the things that need to be done before you begin to sell your product or service.

Business Start-Up Checklist
19 Things to Do Before You Start Your Business

1. Define a Vision and Company Mission Statement
Each business will have core ideals that will remain relatively steady through its existence. These ideals form your vision and will be incorporated into your company's mission statement. Your mission statement will contain three main concepts: the core purpose, the core values and its visionary objectives.

The *core purpose* is the reason your business exists. It can be used to clearly state to your employees and customers why your business operates, other than simply to make money.

Core values are values that are central to your business. These core values will reflect the deeply held values of your company and should not be things that would change over time or if the business changes. Examples of core values are: integrity, creativity, great customer service and social responsibility.

Visionary objectives are clearly defined, lofty milestones that your business will strive to achieve. Unlike strategic or tactical objectives, visionary objectives are "shoot for the sky" type of targets, even though the business may or may not necessarily ever achieve them.

2. Create a business name. This is one of the more fun and creative aspects of the start-up process. But selecting a name is not all fun and games. There could be ramifications to selecting a poor name and well as benefits to selecting a great name. Select a name that is unique and tells your customers what your business does. Your business name will be used to create a first impression as well as to be used as a marketing tool later on.

3. Select a business mailing address. This step, although simple, is necessary in order to complete the business registration processes outlined in the next few steps. If you will be renting an office or starting a retail business these locations will be your business mailing address. If you plan on starting your new business from your home, a suggestion is to use a post office box as your business mailing address, not your home address. This will add credibility to your business.

4. Register your business name. Depending on the city, county and state in which you live there are varying registration requirements for each business. Registering does not necessarily mean "incorporating" a business, although this is one form of registration. It is recommended, but not required, that you do a name search to ensure that no other businesses in your area are using the name you selected. A name search should be done at the local, state and national levels. Although you can do a name search on your own if you are Internet savvy, there are attorneys that specialize in business set-ups and incorporations that can perform this task quickly and relatively inexpensively.

5. Establish a business identity. Forming a legal business entity will help to protect your assets. It will also add credibility to your business as well as create certain tax benefits for you (and your partners.) There are five (5) common, private business entities from which to select. Your business can be a sole proprietorship, a partnership, a C Corporation, a Sub-Chapter "S"

Corporation or a Limited Liability Company (LLC). These different structures are defined at the end of this chapter.

6. Obtain an Employer Identification Number (EIN) from the IRS. An EIN is required if you are planning on hiring employees or incorporate. Securing an EIN from the IRS is a simple process and can be done over the phone, by fax or mail and takes only minutes to complete. This process can also be done by your attorney.

7. Obtain business licenses. Requirements for business licenses vary from state to state, city to city and county to county. These jurisdictions usually require that such licenses are in place before you begin conducting business. You want your business to be in "good legal standing" on the first day you begin transacting business. You can determine what licenses are required in your area by contacting your state, county or city. Each of these has departments that manage the issuance of business licenses. Your attorney can also handle this process for you.

8. Select a business location. Going hand in hand with #3 above (mailing address), select your business location, the place from which your business will operate. If you are not starting your new business from your home, the location you select will be very important especially if it is a retail business. You will need to consider the proper size, the amount of rent you want to pay, the ease of accessibility for clients or the general public, the location of competitors (if applicable), parking, and any other factors that you feel may be important to the future success of your business. Make sure you determine that the property is zoned properly before you sign a lease.

9. Learn about your competition. One of the great success stories in American history is the sale of Japanese autos in the U.S. The Japanese had a very simple philosophy in order to compete with the established U.S. automakers, "Take what already exists and make it better. Do not try to invent a new car." Unless you plan on offering a product that is brand new to the American marketplace, follow this philosophy. Learn about how your competitors have succeeded over the years. Visit their offices or retail locations. Study their marketing and advertising techniques. Search the Internet for similar businesses. Know all about the pricing of their products or services, this will help you to determine appropriate and competitive pricing on your products.

10. Write a business plan. A solid business plan can be a useful guide to running a successful business. It will clearly define your vision and layout a step by step plan to achieving your goals. In a perfect world, it is best to develop a business plan before you launch your business but it is not a requirement. Some entrepreneurs want to get their business up and going as quickly as possible then develop a growth and management plan as a second step. This is personal preference, so here is yet another management decision you will have to make, when to draft and implement a formal business plan.

11. Build and launch a website. Although not essential to all businesses, having a website is fast becoming a necessity for businesses. Having a presence on the web adds credibility but, more important, provides access and information about your business to potential customers not only in your town but around the country and the world. You can build and launch a website relatively inexpensively by doing it yourself, if you are creative. There are many Internet-based companies that provide templates that you can use to construct a site quickly, sometimes even in hours, then offer services to launch the site so it can "go live" on the Internet, as well as to offer the servers necessary on which your site will reside. Websites can also be more than just information; they can offer products for sale through "web stores." If you are selling a product, this may also be another revenue source that you may not have considered.

12. Create a logo. Another fun step in the business start-up process is the creation of a logo. There are software packages out in the marketplace that you can purchase to design your own logo or there are local companies that can do it for you. Your logo will be another representation of your company, so the design and even the colors you select will all be part of how you and your company are perceived in the marketplace. Your logo will subsequently be used on signage, business cards, letterhead, envelopes, and possibly even the products you sell if you will be selling a product that you will be manufacturing yourself.

13. Order business cards and letterhead. Although not a major business step, an important one nonetheless. Your business cards can be used to begin marketing your company to potential clients, they can act as a networking tool, and your letterhead becomes important to follow up with potential clients.

14. Open a business bank account. Under no circumstances should you process business transactions through your personal checking or savings accounts. It costs next to nothing to set up a business checking account at your local bank. Do it! A unique business account will allow you to track your business expenses properly and will also make preparing your tax returns much easier. You will need to have an Employer Identification Number (EIN) in order to open a business bank account, so make sure you complete this step before attempting to open an account.

15. Secure financing to start your business. Not to oversimplify, but it takes money to start and run a business.

a. you can fund it with your own money

b. you can borrow it from a bank (or other lending institution)

c. you can secure venture capital from an outside investor or partner

Each step has advantages and disadvantages. Funding with your own money means you will have less debt to pay back later; however, you will more than likely have to start your operation smaller than you may have imagined. Borrowing money from a bank will require collateral, so although you may be using the bank's money and not your own, you will need appropriate collateral to support the loan. Most entrepreneurs will use the equity in their homes as collateral. If you choose the bank borrowing option, know that it can take as much as three (3) months in order to complete the loan application and approval process with a bank, so plan accordingly. If you want to secure venture capital from an outside investor or potential business partner, you will most certainly need a business plan that clearly defines your business and your business's ability to generate a fair return on investment over a reasonable amount of time. (Make sure you read Chapters 4 and 5, "*Finding Capital to Start a Business*" and "*Red Flags About Business Partners*," respectively.)

16. Insurance. There are several different kinds of insurance that may be necessary to protect your business. If you will have employees, you will need to pay unemployment insurance as well as workers' compensation insurance. Depending on the type of business you select, you may also need product liability insurance if you will be manufacturing your own products and general business liability insurance if you have an office, retail store or manufacturing facility. There are also other insurance types that may be required by your lease such as fire insurance. It is strongly recommended that you speak with an insurance expert prior to starting your business to determine what kinds of insurance your particular business requires, and in what coverage amounts. Insurance premiums will be an ongoing business expense, so plan accordingly.

17. Select an accounting method. There are two (2) basic accounting methods: cash and accrual accounting. Although these will not be discussed in depth here, you will need to decide which method works best for you and your business. You will also need some kind of accounting system to track all of your business transactions. You can do this manually, use accounting software or outsource the entire accounting management process to an accountant. In the Appendix, there is a comparison chart of the different accounting software packages on the market.

18. Have advisors available to provide advice. Entrepreneurs tend to be "A" type personalities that are aggressive and want to do things on their own. Be a little humble and know you cannot have knowledge on how to handle every different business situation that may arise. Have advisors readily available to discuss your business challenges as they arise. Advisors can be family and friends, but may also include an attorney, accountant, banker, or industry experts.

19. Set a Launch Date. Certainly the most exciting part about business preparation is the very last step, actually starting to transact business! Set a date to open your office, store, warehouse or manufacturing facility. If appropriate, make a "big deal" about the opening. Invite family, friends and the general public to an "opening day" ceremony. Contact the press. There is nothing wrong with a little free advertising. Under # 5 above, the book discusses selecting the appropriate business structure for your new enterprise.

Here is a top level definition of the five (5) most common business structures for private companies.

1. Sole Proprietorship. A sole proprietorship is a form of business organization in which an individual is fully and personally liable for all the obligations (including debts) of the business, is entitled to all of its profits, and exercises complete managerial control. The great advantage of operating a new business as a sole proprietorship is that it is simple and does not require any formal action to set it up. You can start your business today as a sole proprietorship. There is no need to wait for an attorney to draft and file documents or for the government to approve them. As a sole proprietor, you are the sole owner of your business.

2. Partnership. A partnership consists of two or more individuals or entities who agree to contribute money, labor, property, or skill to a business and share in its profits, losses, and management. You can have a general partnership or a limited partnership.

A general partnership is made up of investors who manage the business and have unlimited personal liability for its debts.

A limited partnership allows investors who will not be actively involved in the company's operations to become partners without being exposed to unlimited liability for the business' debts, if it should go out of business. Every limited partnership must have at least one general partner and at least one limited partner.

Partners do not need to draft a formal document or undergo any other formality to create a partnership. They should, however, draw up a legal agreement outlining the partners' roles, responsibilities, and signatory rights.

3. C Corporation. If you want to sell shares of stock in your business, consider a C Corporation. All publicly-traded companies are C Corporations which are considered a separate legal entity from the owners (also called the shareholders or stockholders) of the business.

Because of this, the shareholders are not responsible for fees, liabilities and losses associated with the business.

The stock, money and assets earned by the corporation belong to the corporation. Dividends are distributed to shareholders under the direction of the corporation's shareholder-elected Board of Directors. Stockholders then pay taxes on the earned dividends, and the corporation also pays taxes on all profits (known as "double taxation"). To become incorporated, you will fill out the appropriate documents for the state and have all shareholders vote on overall corporate management, stock shares, the name of the company, business industry and other key guidelines.

As a C Corporation you will need to hold annual stockholder meetings and keep meticulous records to avoid legal and accounting problems.

4. Sub-Chapter "S" Corporation. It is possible to avoid the double taxation of a C Corporation by forming an S Corporation. Here, the corporation's income is divided among all of the shareholders who report the earnings on their individual tax returns. This is a tax-efficient way to structure your business if you expect losses in the short term because the individual shareholders can report the losses on their tax returns rather than paying the double taxation of the C Corporation.

The downside is that to become an S Corporation, you must run the company according to a fiscal calendar year, have less than 35 individual stockholders who are all U.S. residents, and have only one class of stock, in addition to other guidelines.

5. Limited Liability Company. A Limited Liability Company (LLC) is a hybrid of a partnership and a corporation. LLCs closely resemble and can be taxed like partnerships or corporations, but, like corporations, offer the benefit of limited liability. LLC owners are shielded from personal liability, and all profits and losses may pass directly to the owners without taxation of the entity itself, depending on the taxation method you select.

Consult your attorney or accountant for which taxation method will work best in your personal situation.

Chapter 5

The Art (and Science) of the Business Plan

A business plan is a written description of your business. It is a document and a tool that describes both what you plan to do and exactly how you plan to do it (with "plan" being the operative word.) A business plan is all about managing a company, not explaining it.

So, if you are planning on starting a business, do you really need a business plan? Aren't your years of experience and industry knowledge really what you need to start and run a successful business? Well, the only person who does not need a business plan is one who is not going into business. Anyone starting a new business or planning on expanding a company where you will consume significant money resources, energy and time, with an expectancy that your company will return a profit, should take the time to draft some kind of plan. If you are of the mind that you do not need a plan, you are effectively telling the world you do not want to plan your business.

Types of Business Plans
There are basically three types of business plans: micro-plans, working plans, and presentation plans. Each requires varying levels of effort, content and presentation.

The Micro-plan. A micro-plan is a business plan overview consisting of no more than ten pages. It includes all of the key elements of a full business plan but with abbreviated attention to the business plan concept, capitalization requirements, pro forma financial statements, cash flow projections, marketing plan, and income projections. A micro-plan can be a great tool to test your business concept with potential investors or partners and to open discussions. A micro-plan can also be used as an outline to develop a full business plan later on.

The Working Plan. A working plan is used to operate a business. It does not have to be formatted with the same level of formality or exactitude as the presentation plan and can exclude certain elements that are not critical to running your business such as the resumes of key personnel or product photographs. However, the key elements that will guide your business from day to day are critically important.

The Presentation Plan. A presentation plan is a working plan on steroids. This plan is used to present your business concept to investors, bankers, companies, and consultants so it will have the highest levels of both content and cosmetics in order to make the strongest possible impression. This plan will also include investor requirements such as due diligence on competitors and an analysis of threats and risks to the business. A presentation plan will include charts, graphs and photographs which do not necessarily need to be part of the working plan. Most important, the information contained in a presentation plan must be accurate and consistent. Outside readers will be completely unsympathetic to errors. Such errors may be construed as an intentional misrepresentation or incompetence. It is very rare to get a second chance at presenting your business concept, so your presentation must be first rate, impressive but most of all, accurate and realistic.

Elements of a Business Plan
There are generally accepted guidelines to follow when developing a good business plan relative to both form and content. A business plan has three main parts:

1. Business Concept. In this section, you discuss your product or service, the industry, the general business structure and your plans on how to make the business successful and profitable. Contained in this section are the: Executive Summary and Business Description.

2. Marketplace Section. In this section, you discuss your competition in detail and the ways in which you will compete to gain market share; you analyze and describe potential customers, where they come from, their buying habits, potential for repeat sales, expansion into new markets, etc. Contained in this section are the: Marketing Plan, Competitive Analysis, Design and Development Plan, and the Operations and Management Plan.

3. Financial Section. In this section, you present the financial reports essential to running your new business.

Important note: *Many potential investors and bankers will immediately bypass the Business Concept and Marketplace sections and focus on the financial section first. Their primary interest in your business is to make money. If the financial section is accurate and shows a reasonable return on investment, investors will then go back and start reading about the business concept and how you plan to achieve success.*

Contained in this section are: pro forma income statements, balance sheet, cash flow statement, breakeven analysis, capital budget, operating budget, marketing budget, and payroll analysis.

In addition to these sections, a business plan should also have a cover, title page, table of contents, and appendices.

Length of a Business Plan

Business plans can vary in length depending on the complexity of the business and the intended use of the plan. Plans can be as few as 10 pages and as many as 100 pages, but average plans tend to be 15 to 20 pages in length.

If you are trying to raise large sums of money to launch your new enterprise, say a million dollars or more, your plan will need to be longer and contain as much detail as possible. Conversely, if the plan is meant to manage the day to day operations of a small business, it will be considerably smaller and less detailed. Regardless of how you plan to use your business plan, take care that the content is correct and accurately represents your plans and business expectations. Investors and bankers are professionals who review business plans all the time. Inaccurate or misleading information will be spotted and highlighted and may reflect poorly on you and your ability to plan and run a business successfully.

Investors are grounded in reality. Do not present a plan that shows millions of dollars of sales and profits after one year believing that an investor will be so impressed with your company's potential that he cannot pass up this opportunity. Ensure that your plan reflects not only your business's capabilities but yours as well as a grounded, industry-knowledgeable entrepreneur who is willing to work hard and follow a plan to ensure long term success.

Chapter 6

Finding Capital to Start a Business

There are many elements to starting a new company and you are slowly but surely getting a handle on all of the things you need to do to launch your new business. You have identified a good product or service to sell. There is a market demand or your product or service will provide a solution of some kind to consumers or to business. You have plenty of experience in your area and have put together a reasonable business plan to help guide you through the early stages of your business. You have researched the kind of technology that you need to run your business, identified a few key positions for your team, and have a competent attorney and accountant ready to provide support services. The last big step is to find sufficient capital to launch and run your business.

Unfortunately, this is going to be the single biggest and most challenging obstacle in the new business process. Raising capital is not an easy task regardless of how prepared you are to run a business. In this chapter we will discuss some of the obstacles new entrepreneurs face in seeking ways to fund their new business ideas and address many of the misconceptions about raising capital. There will be a focus on two (2) of the more common methods of start-up financing, bootstrapping and angel investors.

Let's begin with a dose of reality and address some of the major misconceptions about funding for small businesses. Obtaining sufficient capital to start and run a business is not an easy task; in fact, it will be the single most difficult, time consuming task in the new start-up process. You will experience rejection and criticism about your new business idea that you may not anticipate, and if you believe you will raise money quickly, you will soon become frustrated and disillusioned with the process and begin to reconsider if you should even continue down the entrepreneur road. However, if you approach the capital raising function of starting a new business knowledgeable of what is to come, you can manage your time and frustration levels, become more expert in making presentations, and eventually you will succeed in raising the money you need to finally get your new business started.

Misconceptions abound among potential entrepreneurs about capitalizing small businesses. Here are some of the more common ones, so do not fall into the trap of believing any of them.

Misconception # 1: *"I don't need a business plan. I can explain every aspect of my business to anyone at anytime."*

The Facts: According to the U.S. Small Business Administration (SBA), approximately 90% of start-up businesses fail within one (1) year. The great majority of those businesses that fail also never had a business plan. Additionally, if you have plans to grow your business to any size, statistics show that of all new start-up businesses only 5% will ever achieve $1 million in annual revenue. Of that 5% that reaches the $1 million revenue mark, only 2% of those companies will ever reach $5 million in annual revenue. If you want to grow your business to generate not only enough revenue (and subsequently profit) to live comfortably but to also plan for your retirement, you will need to plan. Further, if you intend on raising capital from outside sources, investors will require a well-defined business plan. Put the work in on the front end, develop a business plan, use it as a tool to start and run your business, and update it, as needed, to adjust your business as circumstances change.

Misconception # 2: *"There are many funding sources available in the U.S. so I will be able to secure funding for my new business in a short period of time."*

Facts: Although the first part of the misconception is true, the process of actually identifying a proper funding source and securing that funding can sometimes take years. A good entrepreneur will research the market and target his energies toward potential investors that invest in like companies. For example, if you are starting a technology services company, do not solicit investors who predominantly seek out biotech companies into which they invest their money. This will lead to a much higher rejection rate. Have a well-defined business plan particularly the financial section. This may come as a surprise, but many investors will immediately turn to the financial section of a business plan before even reading about what your company is all about. Investors are about one thing only, and that one thing is not your dream. It is about ROI (return on investment). Know this term, what it means and the importance to investors. People with liquidity that have the ability to invest in companies are looking for opportunities that will generate an ROI greater than if they invest their money into real estate, the stock market or government bonds. They are also looking at the security of their investment, how to mitigate risk and how long it will take to generate the desired return. Investors are interested in the business profit proposition. Your concept is truly secondary.

Misconception # 3: *"I have a great product or idea. Everyone will want to invest."*

Facts: No they won't. Having a great idea or product is certainly necessary, and your enthusiasm and passion about your business will take you a long way, particularly when it comes time to sell; however, true investors will care very little about your passion or your concept if the numbers don't pan out. Investors will acknowledge your experience and passion and must be comfortable investing in you as well as the business concept, but the reality is that most will not want to invest in your company for one reason or another. Do not be disappointed. To investors, your business is not personal as it is to you. There is an old expression that may put this in context, "I don't love it until I own it." This is especially true of investors. Your opportunity is a business transaction only as they seek a substantial return on their investment. If an investor does not see the return potential, there will be no investment; but there will be a total disregard for your great idea. Conversely, if an investor does choose to take the leap and invest in your new business, he will then become a great asset sharing his relationships and knowledge about building a successful business. Remember, he probably has done it before, so he will become a great resource and will begin sharing your passion. The trick is to get him in first.

Misconception # 4: *"Contacting many investors will increase my chances of securing funding."*

Facts: Securing an investor is a form of selling. If you are going to sell apples, would you send out mass mailings and e-mail blasts to every business in the country? Of course not. This will be an incredible waste of time and money. You will want to target your sales approach to those people or businesses that have a need for apples such as grocery stores or simply people that like to eat apples. The same is true for finding investors. The process should be well thought out and focus on quality not quantity. You want your approach to be targeted and personal. Seek out investors who have knowledge about your industry or have a history of investing in like companies. They will have a much higher probability of understanding what it is you are trying to achieve and will be able to assist you if they decide to invest. Do not use form letters but personalized letters specifically addressed to each investor. Keep in mind that investors have many opportunities from which to select. Yours must stand out to be considered. Showing a high level of professionalism in your letter writing with clear, concise language that outlines your request will make a great first impression and increase your chances of getting an audience.

Misconception # 5: *"I can get funding from the Small Business Administration (SBA)."*

Fact: This is one of the more common misconceptions of entrepreneurs. First, the SBA does not loan money, it guarantees loans made by lending institutions to small businesses. Second, the reality (even though they will not admit it) is that SBA loans are used to stimulate minority business ownership. Historically, women and African Americans have had the greatest success in securing loans, and middle-aged, white males find rejection to be the norm. Anecdotally, I personally have had bankers tell me to not even waste my time with the SBA advising me that the likelihood of loan approval is almost zero. On the other hand, if you are a woman or have minority status in the U.S., the SBA might be a good source, but keep in mind that SBA loans tend to be small and will more than likely be insufficient to support your business plan. Regardless, every little bit helps and if you are able to secure an SBA loan that will go a long way in showing other potential investors that you are in good standing with the U.S. government, that your credit is good, that another entity recognizes your value proposition and that there is a reasonable belief that you will have the ability to repay a loan. These are all positives to potential investors.

Misconception # 6: *"Venture capitalists will want to invest in my company."*

Facts: There is a difference between a venture capitalist and an angel investor which will be discussed in more depth later on in this chapter. A venture capitalist traditionally invests in existing companies with clear revenue and cash flow streams. Their investments are less risky and speculative. Venture capitalists usually take more aggressive ownership positions in companies because investments tend to be larger. Most venture firms will not even consider small investments (i.e., $500,000 or less). Venture capital is almost always comprised of money from multiple investors with the firm managing the investment process, therefore, a venture capital firm is very selective about investing funds because they have many investors funding their investment "pool" that require explanations. Conversely, angel investors are single people, men or women, who entertain more risk and are more likely to consider a start-up venture.

Misconception # 7: *"I can get money from government grants."*

Facts: Almost all government grants are for companies that fall into one of four categories: educational, scientific, not-for-profit or medical. Grants also tend to be small and will not be sufficient to start or run a new business. If your new business falls into one of these four categories, know that the grant process is highly competitive with limited funds to be awarded and many, many applicant companies being considered. If you feel grants are a potential source of capital for your new enterprise, consider grant sources in additional to those offered by the Federal government. These other sources can include states, private companies and foundations.

Seven Types of Funding Sources

Seven types of funding will be outlined below with a focus on two in particular, bootstrapping and angel investors. It goes without saying that properly financing your new company will be a critical element in its success. The single greatest reason why new businesses have such a high failure rate is undercapitalization. Do everything you can to be properly funded before launching your new business. Here are your options:

Bootstrapping

In simplest terms, "bootstrapping" is funding your new company yourself using your savings, credit cards, home equity, kids' college fund (which I do not recommend), 401(k), pension plans, or other personally controlled sources.

Pros:

- You maintain complete financial and operational control over your business.
- There are no equity-holders or lenders to pay off.
- You will not have monthly loan principal and interest payments as part of your business expenses.

Cons:

- Your personal assets are at risk.
- Depending on the source of your personal capital, you will pay a high interest rate if you use credit card advances, or you will lose earning interest income if you use savings.
- Typically, this form of funding limits the amount of money you have for strategic purposes and the rate of growth of your business can be

significantly slowed down as it struggles with cash flow.

Bootstrapping is funding your new business personally while keeping your operating expenses to a minimum. When you bootstrap a business, you learn very quickly about money management because you are funding the company with your own resources. People tend to learn very quickly about money management when they use their own money as opposed to someone who starts out with a large investment of someone else's cash.

Externally funded businesses are often misled into believing they are running a successful business because they are able to pay rents and salaries, but the bootstrapper knows that a business needs paying customers in order to survive. When you fund a company on your own, you will be very customer focused because you learn very quickly that the only other source of cash is from those very customers. Bootstrappers also tend to build very cost-efficient operations, never wasting money and minimizing expenses wherever they can to keep positive cash flow, if possible.

If you are going to consider bootstrapping your new company, here are some pointers to focus on to increase your chances of success:

1. **Work on establishing good credit with suppliers and your bank.**

2. **Keep your operating costs down.** Every dime you spend reduces your cash flow and your ability to succeed.

3. **Do it yourself.** If there are things to be done, do them yourself if you can. Do not hire people unnecessarily. If you do not know how to do something, study. It will cost you less money in the short and long runs.

4. **Get things done.** Do not dwell on doing every task perfectly. You will learn what to do and not to do over time. It is more important to be a little reckless and get things done even if they are not perfect.

5. **Do not exclude external investors.** Although you are starting out using your own money, as your business grows you may find a need for additional capital to expand, hire people, buy inventory or advertise. It will be a little easier to secure external funding for an existing business compared to a start-up particularly if your business is profitable with positive cash flow.

Angel Investors

Angel investors are individuals who invest in start-up or early stage companies in exchange for equity, debt or some combination thereof. Generally, "angels" look to invest anywhere from $25,000 to $1 million of their own money. They are usually successful businesspeople who will be able to also provide to you advice in addition to money.

Pros:

- Angels invest money, expertise, experience, and networking contacts

- Angels tend to be patient about receiving a return on their investment

- Usually, an angel's investment into a company is in the form of equity (as opposed to debt) meaning they will make their profits when the company shows a profit or when you choose to sell the business.

Cons:

- Angels can be difficult to find. You want to seek out angels that have knowledge about your business or industry, so they can provide ongoing advice and support.

- Angels expect regular reporting. These reports will be not only monthly financial statements but sales reports, operations, inventory or other forms of reporting specific to your business.

- Angels receive an equity position in your company. This means that you are not the sole owner of the company, and with ownership comes rights and control.

How to Pitch the Rich

If you truly want to succeed in partnering with a wealthy individual, here are 8 rules to follow to avoid common mistakes often made by first-time pitchers.

1. Be prepared with a first class business plan. Before you even meet with an angel investor, you need to have a first class business plan. He will ask to see it. Without it, your meeting will be cut short and you may not get a second chance. You must be prepared to show the angel that you have a well thought out plan for starting and running a business. As discussed in several prior areas in this book, the financial section of the business plan will be key. If you are a start-up business, you must have the following elements in the financial section: a forecasted balance sheet, 3 to 5 year forecasted income statement, 3 to 5 year cash flow plan, and a breakeven analysis. Without a business plan, do not even have the meeting.

2. The "Elevator Pitch." An elevator pitch is a 30 second verbal description of your business and its financial needs. You must be able to explain your business to an angel investor in this time to start the meeting. From this point, the angel will begin asking questions or wanting you to expand on certain concepts in your business plan. Do not make your introductory speech long, cumbersome and with a lot of detail. Keep in mind that the angel is not familiar with your business concept and it will not impress him by dumping minute fact after fact on him. He will start to get confused, bored and lose interest. Investors are interested in businesses that will attract and retain customers, as well as show positive cash flow. If the angel gets confused, he will assume your customers will also be confused and he will conclude that your concept is simply not well thought out.

3. The Executive Summary. As a separate document, have a short Executive Summary. An Executive Summary is a 2 to 4 page document that summarizes your business plan. It is a snapshot of your business concept, its investment needs, and its financial forecast. Be prepared for the angel to ask for an Executive Summary before you even have a chance to say word one. Without it, you will be perceived as being unprepared. Some angels prefer to read an Executive Summary to understand the business concept and needs before engaging in a discussion.

4. Be humble. Take the position that you are not the smartest person in the room. Arrogance seldom impresses investors. Know what you know and what you don't know and do not be afraid to admit it. Acknowledge that the investor is successful and that he has value beyond his money. If your business plan specifically targets the angel's company as a perspective client, do not tell him how much he needs you to solve all of his business problems with your product or service. The reality is he doesn't. Angels are looking for people that have a grasp on reality. Angels will also focus on a section of the business plan that discusses the management team. If you plan on growing an enterprise, you will have to articulate what kinds of management personnel you will need, and the strengths they will add to the company. An angel must be comfortable that his investment will be protected and managed properly.

5. Respect his time. If you have a meeting scheduled with an investor, be on time. Do not expect to stay longer than your allotted time. Make sure your presentation is completed on time. If you are asked to stay longer, that is the investor's choice. Approach the meeting like it is not only your first but your last. Often times, you get one shot at an investor.

6. Be conservative. Although you may be passionate and excited about your business and truly believe that it is a multi-million idea, do not make wild income predictions over short periods of time. As a consultant, I have heard new entrepreneurs make presentations to investors telling them their new business will generate $100 million revenue per year in less than five (5) years. No it won't and investors know that. Pie-in-the-sky forecasting will not impress investors, it will show them you do not have a grasp on reality and probably do not truly understand your business, the marketplace or your competitors well enough to be seriously considered. Avoid graphs and charts showing sales and profit lines going straight up into the air and off the chart. Know that investors are savvy business people that understand that new businesses need to start off slow, develop cost-efficient operations, build customers then make profits (in that order). Do not show an investor that your company will be making profits after only a few months because it is unlikely that it will. Show the angel that you have a well thought out plan for controlled growth, fiscal constraint and profitability after a "reasonable" amount of time.

7. Know your competitors. Every good entrepreneur needs to know their competition and the marketplace. Smart investors will certainly ask, *"Tell me about your competitors and why you believe your product offering is better than theirs."* Do not answer this question with a polite answer such as, *"Well, I don't really want to badmouth my competition."* Not only does this response not answer the question but the angel never asked you to badmouth anyone. This type of response will be perceived as you not knowing anything about your competition and a strong negative in the presentation. You need to know everything about your competitors or at least as much as you can, including their products, pricing and methods of distribution. Your business plans on invading their market space so you need to explain to the angel why you believe customers will buy your product over your competitor's product. Understanding the marketplace and your competitors will be a very strong positive. Investors are hard to fool, so do not try. If you get caught, your opportunity will be gone.

8. Present facts not fiction. Impress your investor with your knowledgeable fact base. Do not make stuff up about customers, buying behaviors, market demand and especially financial projections. For example, if you plan on selling widgets in your local area and the largest widget dealer generates $1 million per year, do not forecast widget sales of $10 million per year in the same marketplace. Understand the market, and where you believe you can position your company within it. Present facts about your work experiences and how they may be relevant to running this new business.

9. Take notes. Taking notes is a sign of respect for what an investor has to say. It will not be perceived as offensive or not paying attention. Do not ask an investor to repeat names, numbers, or statistics and do not try to commit these types of things to your memory. An angel might ask you to do certain things in preparation for another meeting. You need to be sure to complete ALL of those things, not only the ones you can remember. By accurately completing research or tasks, this will signal that you are responsive and follow through when things need to be done. This is a positive in the angel's decision making process.

Family and Friends

Next to using your own money, family and friends can be a resource. However, there are certainly pros and cons to borrowing money from these two groups. Investing by family and friends can be in the form of either equity or debt (stock ownership or loans.)

Pros:

- You are a known entity
- Funds are usually available fairly quickly
- Fewer contractual constraints (although you should certainly do everything by the book when borrowing from friends and family so all parties understand their obligations, risks and returns)
- More readily available to help run your business, if needed

Cons:

- Funding is usually a one-time event and often in limited amounts
- Business failure and your inability to repay a loan may have personal relationship consequences

Debt Financing

If you are truly a start-up business, it is unlikely that you will qualify for debt financing. Debt financing requires the use of a traditional bank loan or a loan guaranteed by the SBA. Business loans put a great deal of weight on existing operations, particularly cash flow, which is a key indicator as to whether or not a business has the ability to pay back a loan. Because a start-up business has no sales or cash flow, it is not likely that a bank will grant a loan simply on a business plan unless you have the ability to personally guarantee or collateralize a loan.

Pros:

- You do not give up equity or control of all or part of your company
- You begin building a strong relationship with a banker that you may need down the road as your business expands and new loans or lines of credit need to be established

Cons:

- Loans have interest payments, so this cost will be added to your normal operating expenses
- Not paying loans and/or interest payments on time can have severe consequences on your

business's credit rating and future ability to borrow funds

- Loans may require personal guarantees or substantial collateral

Venture Capitalists

Venture capitalists do not typically invest in start-up companies. If you are an entrepreneur to be, venture capital is not a true option. Unlike angel investors who tend to be wealthy individuals, venture capitalists usually represent a pool of money collected from multiple investors. A venture capital firm manages the process of investing these funds into existing companies, often times to acquire companies. If, by chance, you own an existing company that is at least two (2) years old and you are looking to expand or possibly sell your company, a venture capital firm might be an option. Venture capital firms vary in size and investment capability with investments ranging from $250,000 to tens of millions of dollars or more. There is also expectancy for high, rapid growth and a fast return on investment.

Pros:

- VCs offer more than just funding, often providing management expertise as well as networking capabilities
- VCs typically have additional funds available, if necessary, down the road

Cons:

- VCs often require significant operating control in your company
- VCs typically only invest in established companies
- VCs require a well-defined exit strategy or IPO plan (IPO means initial public offering or taking a company public after a certain period of time)

Grants

Grants are special programs funded through local, state or federal governments or through private foundations. Grants are designed to support certain types of businesses such as minority-owned businesses, not-for-profits, medical research, educational or technology driven businesses.

Pros:

- Grants are not loans. They can be defined as "free money." There is no requirement to pay back grant money or to even pay interest on the funds.
- Investors perceive grant revenue as a strong positive incentive to invest additional funds.

Cons:

- There is a great deal of competition for grant money
- Grant writing is a skill. Employ or contract with someone who is expert in this function if it is something you choose to pursue
- The use of grant money is usually very strictly defined by the organization or government agency that provides the funds

Factoring

Factoring is a lending process by a financial institution whereby it advances money against proceeds from the company's outstanding accounts receivables. Factors are generally paid a percentage of the future invoices, when collected. Similar to debt financing, factoring is only applicable to businesses that have existing accounts receivables, so this would not be applicable to new start-ups.

Pros:

- Improves company's cash flow
- Funds availability quickly

Cons:

- Greater accounting, oversight and administration
- Very high fees associated with factoring
- Customers making payments to a factoring company or bank, not your company

You are now ready to take on the most challenging part of starting a new business, the financing part. Follow the simple guidelines outlined in this chapter and your chances of securing financing will be greatly improved. Learn as much as you can about your business, including your competitors. Translate all of your knowledge to a well-written business plan including a concise Executive Summary. Keep your presentations short, to the point and driven by facts, not speculation. You may believe that you may have a multi-million idea, but be conservative in your business planning and when presenting to investors. It is great to be confident, but do not be arrogant. Show you are a grounded individual that is honest, sincere and knowledgeable with realistic expectations for growth and profitability. And most important, know your numbers! You absolutely must have a solid grasp of the finances of your business when presenting to investors. If you do not, your meeting with be short-lived and unproductive. For investors, it is all about the ROI. If you remember anything in this chapter, remember that.

Chapter 7

Red Flags about Business Partners

You are now at the point when becoming an entrepreneur is seriously being considered. You have found a great product or service, you have tested the marketplace and believe you have a market to sell to, you have honestly evaluated your strengths and weaknesses, you are evaluating how much money you might need to start and run your new enterprise, and you have spoken to experts about what kind of business you would like to start. You are working diligently to learn about running a business and become an industry expert in your field.

But during the process of honestly evaluating your strengths and weakness, you have identified certain weaknesses that could be detrimental to your new business. So, how will you solve this dilemma? There are several solutions:

First, you can begin by studying about those areas that you do not feel knowledgeable enough to handle on your own. You could go back to school and put off the start of your business until you secure the expertise necessary to run all aspects of your business. In some cases, this might be a very good idea, if you can afford it. There may be a need, more than a desire, to start this new venture, so waiting a year or two to become educated might not be an equitable solution.

Second, another alternative is to simply hire people that are expert in the areas in which you feel less knowledgeable. For example, maybe the business you are thinking about starting requires inventory management. You have no experience in buying inventory or running a warehouse, you don't know anything about fulfillment operations, inventory turns, shelf lives, and so many other things about inventory control, picking and packing, or WMS (warehouse management systems.) However, one of the things you have learned about starting a business is to control your expenses, so hiring people that are expert in warehouse and fulfillment operations could be an expensive proposition, especially when you have no sales to support these costs. In addition, although they will be knowledgeable, you will be responsible for managing them, which creates a whole new set of responsibilities. Managing people is both an art and a science, and to take on the task of managing new employees that know much more than you in certain areas of your business will be a challenge you may not necessarily want to take on at the outset of your new enterprise.

Third, you can forge ahead regardless of what you don't know. Someone invented the expression, "Learn as you go," so why not do it that way. This is certainly an option; however, this option increases your risk of making errors. In the example cited where you may need to run a warehouse and fulfillment operation as an integral part of your business, this may very well be the single highest cost area in your company when you consider warehouse space lease costs, equipment, employees, utilities, and of course, the inventory itself. Inventory buying requires a high level of expertise because to stock warehouse shelves in advance of orders means money is going out and no money is coming in, so cash management becomes an essential element in this process. (Oh, yes, you don't know anything about cash management either.)

Fourth, you can outsource the whole operation. Certainly an option and many start-up and small companies do exactly this to avoid having to manage employees, inventory control, fulfillment, pilferage, and reporting. However, this is also another cost that you are trying to manage and you will certainly pay a premium for a professional inventory control company to manage this part of your business. In addition, you may find some resistance from these companies because your new business may be too small for them to effectively manage to a profit.

So, you consider Option 5, bringing in a business partner. On its face, it seems like a wonderful solution, to find a person that knows all about inventory management and fulfillment operations, give him an equity position in your new business, possibly even secure a cash investment from the new partner to help finance the business, and then you can do what you do best and he can manage the warehouse and fulfillment side of the business. Seems like a perfect solution!

However, business partnerships are much like marriages. There are great partners, good partners and then very bad partners and we all know what happens when you have a bad partner. Your new business can turn into a day to day hell, you may have to consider dissolving the company because you simply can't work together, or worse, you could wind up in court suing each other.

My own personal observations are that for every successful partnership there are 100 poor ones. Remember, if this is something you are seriously going to consider, you are not only solving a work expertise problem but you will have to trust your financial security to someone else. Now this someone else may be someone you know or do not know. So, the million dollar question becomes, "Are you ready to gamble your business and financial security on someone else's character, business knowledge, personality and work ethic?"

The word "gamble" was chosen carefully and with thought. According to dictionary.com some of the definitions of the word "gamble" are:

1. to bet on an uncertain outcome
2. to take a risk in the hope of gaining an advantage or a benefit
3. to engage in reckless or hazardous behavior
4. to expose to hazard or risk
5. To stake or risk money or anything of value on the outcome of something involving chance
6. any matter or thing involving risk or hazardous uncertainty

Here is a list of the worst possible partners for your new start-up business and some tips on how to avoid making a disastrous mistake. So, in the tradition of that wonderful 90's sitcom, *Seinfeld*, let's give everyone potential partner a pet name to keep them easy to remember.

The "Procrastinator"

The Procrastinator is someone that talks the talk but does not walk the walk. Whatever needs to get done today will not be done but dubiously pledged to be done tomorrow (or next week or next month.) You can have meeting after meeting to define the urgency of actions, you can plan, set objectives and timelines, but there will always be reasons why things cannot get done on time or ever for that matter. His personal mantra is "put off today what you can do tomorrow" unfortunately, it will not get done tomorrow because as we all know "tomorrow never comes." When starting a new business, it will be all about getting things done correctly, on time or ahead of schedule. Avoid a partner with a history of slow response times. You want a partner who is a "doer," someone who will be a self-starter. Remember, it is easier to pull back someone than to push them.

The "Perfectionist"

Similar to the Procrastinator, the Perfectionist will also never get anything done but for a completely different set of reasons. No decisions will be made because of a fear of making a wrong decision, so his modus operandi will be to work every decision to death, to do endless research, to consult experts, to call friends, to build spreadsheets. Although as an entrepreneur you want to minimize making mistakes, it will be more important to actually do things to move your business forward so it can grow. You will learn from your mistakes, if necessary. If you read about successful entrepreneurs, they have many characteristics in common, one of which is a willingness to take risks. You hear that all the time. Taking risks translates to taking action. Of course you always want to make the best possible decisions based on as much good information as possible, but you still need to make decisions without a fear of making mistakes. Create your best possible plan and implement it today. Do not fall into the trap that tomorrow's plan will be perfect. It will not.

The "Sheep"

The "Sheep" may be an acceptable partner under certain circumstances. The Sheep is a follower. She is an expert at working 40 hours per week, collecting a paycheck, doing her job well, looking for her cost of living adjustment at the end of the year, and being home by 6 p.m. to have dinner. She does not work weekends. One percent of Americans are leaders the other 99% are followers. This doesn't mean they are bad people, in fact, there are many, many fabulous employees throughout the country, but will they make great business partners? If you want a partner that will take direction well and probably get things done when you ask, the Sheep may be a good choice. But, if you are looking for a leader to take on big responsibility in your new company, take the proverbial bull by the horns, make decisions, provide expertise that you may not have and act on it, The Sheep will be a bad choice because she will always be looking for direction from you. Remember the example of the warehouse and fulfillment operation that your new business requires? Well, if you partner with The Sheep with the expectancy for her to jump in, build and run the fulfillment operation while you manage the company's sales and finances, it will not happen. There will be endless phone calls and emails about what to do next. Unfortunately, you don't know anything about running a warehouse, so you will most likely provide poor direction that will lead to bad decisions. Bad decisions will ultimately cost you money. Hire the Sheep; don't take her in as a partner.

The "Inventor"
The Inventor is just that, an inventor. Have no expectations that anyone that is an inventor knows or even cares about how to run a business. Inventors are often brilliant, creative people and sometimes they actually can develop a product that has market value. They know about electronics, engineering, software applications, technology, injection molding, soldering and all sorts of technical things, but do not know or care anything about the "P" word, "profit." Although they all want to become rich by inventing and selling some new and innovative product, in their perfect world, they want to be in the lab creating the next super widget and anything that has to do with sales, marketing, manufacturing, finances or human resources really needs to be handled by someone else. If you come across a new product developed by an Inventor, there are many ways to have a successful relationship with the Inventor, one of which is not as a partner. Acquire the rights to manufacture and sell his product, make him a supplier, keep him at arms' length. Have no expectancy that the Inventor will help you to build and run your business. He will not. In his mind he is a creative genius and cannot be bogged down with any

element of running a business other than building a lab and inventing the next great thing.

The "Fantasist"

The Fantasist is someone not grounded in reality but rather lives in the future. She has big dreams of what life will be like in the future with no idea about how to achieve those dreams. She will talk about the million dollar house, the Bentley, retiring at 39, owning the chalet in Aspen, and traveling the world after you make tons of money from your new business. The problem with this partner is a small little obstacle called hard work for 10 or 20 years before those dreams even start to become a reality. Unfortunately, this is not part of the Fantasist's plan for untold riches. People that live for the future don't do well in the present, so have no expectancy for hard work to be a contribution of this dreamer. Just for the record, there is absolutely nothing wrong with wanting to accumulate wealth and have all of the wonderful things life has to offer. It may have been part of your personal life plan that you detailed when you first began thinking about starting a business. The difference is you know that you will have to work long and hard to achieve success, the Fantasist does not. It is also very likely that she will also not have a clue about how to achieve any of the company's objectives because if she did, she would already be rich and retired. Dream big but partner with someone that is skilled and knows there is a long road of hard work in front of them.

The "Donald"
The Donald makes reference to billionaire, Donald Trump. Mr. Trump loves to spend money on lavish surroundings, hiring top executives, traveling in private jets, and eating at the finest restaurants. He is an entrepreneur that has built many successful businesses and lives a life reaping the rewards of his success. Certain personalities equate owning a business with extravagant spending. Stay away from The Donald personality type when looking for a partner. He will want a large, fancy office, convince you that your new company should lease cars for the both of you, travel first class, buy letterhead with gold foil and live the lifestyle of the real Donald regardless of the business's ability to support such a lifestyle. Look for a partner who is a fiscal conservative, that wants to not only make a profit but to make as much profit as possible by controlling costs. Companies that make profit can then reinvest into their future by hiring more employees,

upgrading equipment and software, buying more inventory or expanding into new sales markets. If you allow The Donald to spend the company's money on non-essential items there will be no opportunity to reinvest into your company when the time comes for expansion. If you have no money for expansion, you either don't expand or... well, you will need another partner to invest some working capital into your company, and then you will have to read this chapter all over again about bringing in new partners. I don't think you want to go through this process twice.

The "Chief"
The Chief is someone regardless of her official title in the company will act like its Chief Executive Officer (CEO). Even if she is a minority partner owning only 10% of the business, the Chief will be expert at giving directions to employees, putting herself out in public as the CEO (in fact or in fiction), talking about how successful the company is whether it is true or not. She is an expert at puffery. Unfortunately, people with "chief syndrome" are expert at giving direction and usually very poor at actually doing work. Stay away from egotistical maniacs. The bigger and more successful your business becomes, the bigger the ego

will become and this will inevitably lead to conflict because the Chief will be quick to take credit for the company's success and be ready to blame others, including you, for its failures.

The "Illusionist"

When you think of an illusionist, what do they do best? The answer is "disappear." After becoming a partner, have no expectancy to ever see your partner again. He will always be somewhere else and never available to work. If he does come to work, expect him to take long lunches or be leaving early. By definition, this is what he does. He creates the illusion of working. Avoid this personality at all costs unless you love asking the question, "Where is Bob?" He will be here today, gone tomorrow or here today and gone today. When you do find him, do not be surprised if he is on vacation halfway across the country. One of the keys to running a successful business is productivity, getting the most out of every employee and yourself. If The Illusionist is not there to work there will be zero productivity and no productivity has a direct cost impact on your company's profits. This personality is better suited to be an apprentice for David Copperfield.

The "Money Pit"

Remember the movie, *The Money Pit*, starring Tom Hanks and Shelley Long? It is a movie about a young couple that buys an old house where they continually have to invest money repairing things that are wrong with the house. Avoid the Money Pit partner. This is someone who has an endless need for money. He is unlike The Donald who wants to spend money extravagantly. Instead, The Money Pit partner "needs" to spend money on auto repairs, the kids' college education, credit card debt and all sorts of other personal problems. A great candidate for this title is the divorcee who is also responsible for alimony and child support payments. The Money Pit partner will see the company as a money well that can be used to solve his personal problems on a moment's notice. You and your business are not a bank that can be run to whenever there is a financial crisis. When considering a partner, interview potential candidates as you would an employee, but unlike an employee interview ask about the potential partner's personal life, financial situation, how they see the role of the business in their life. All questions are fair game in a partnership interview. You are not bound by Federal laws regarding fair employment practices. You have a right to know everything there is to know about your potential partner, so do not be afraid to ask. Lack of knowledge will not be a credible defense when your business fails because your new partner withdrew or borrowed all of the equity out of your new company.

The "Drinking Buddy"
The Drinking Buddy is the partner conceived in a drunken stupor. We have all been there sitting in a bar, drinking, and the great ideas start to flow. Sometimes these ideas are even written down on a nearby napkin and stuck in your pocket. Lucky for you that napkins are not (necessarily) legally binding documents. The Drinking Buddy will share all of her ideas about empire building, changing the world and becoming rich; but after the hangover, your buddy needs to get back to work and that if you want to start the company based on your bar conversation have at it. You can always give her a call for more drunken advice, but do not expect her to be around to run a company. Just don't forget to send a check for her half of the profits each month. Partnering with The Drinking Buddy will have you earning half the profits in return for all of the work. There is a business term for this, "inequitable."

Now that we have identified certain personality types who would make poor partners, what if you truly have a need for a partner? What should you do to find the perfect business partner? Partners can fall into several different categories relative to equity sharing. What this means is that if you elect to have a partner that person does not necessarily have to be an equal partner.

Partnerships can be challenging, especially equal partners. There are advantages and disadvantages associated with the varying degrees of partnerships. In a partnership where there are only two partners (there can be more), partners may be equal with each owning or controlling 50% of the company. One partner may have a controlling interest of 51% to 66% with the other partner having the reciprocal amount. Or, one partner may control more than 67% of the company's voting rights. Legally, each situation has its own unique ramifications on who has what authority in making decisions for the company. This book is not going to delve into the legal aspects of shareholder rights. In the chapter titled, "What to do BEFORE You Start a Business," there is a top level discussion about selecting a competent attorney as part of the set-up process. Your attorney will be able to clearly explain to you the rights and responsibilities of partners and can assist you in preparing an Operating Agreement that will govern behaviors.

This chapter is dedicated to finding the perfect business partner. Earlier, a comparison was made between a business and a marriage. In each, there must be a reliance on the other to protect one another's interests and financial security. Each must contribute work. You will need to be able to trust your partner, be able to communicate openly and honestly, resolve problems, face financial challenges, deal with employees, vendors and clients, and make major decisions together.

Here are some helpful tips to consider when searching for that perfect partner:

First, decide what kind of partner you need. The basic areas of most businesses are sales, finance and accounting, marketing, information technology, operations, engineering and manufacturing (for product manufacturing), warehouse and fulfillment (if applicable), business development, human resources, customer service, and capitalization. Determine what skill set you bring to your company then look for a partner that will compliment your talents, meaning his skills will be those things at which you are weakest.

Besides skills and experience, you must also look for a partner that will be a good personality match. Look for a partner whose demeanor, temperament, business ethics and work habits fit well with yours.

Second, network to find the right partner. Seek out industry experts for recommendations. Speak with past business colleagues particularly if you are starting a business similar to the one in which you may have worked. Consider former co-workers if you found you worked well with them in another environment. Network with friends and relatives for recommendations. Seek out professionals for advice such as bankers, attorneys and accountants regarding potential partners.

Third, be selective. The ability for a partner to invest money should not be the only criteria used to measure a partner's potential, although it may be a very important element. Like in a marriage, a partner needs to be someone you like, respect, has similar goals and aspirations, similar business philosophies and with ethics, character and integrity. Do not settle for a partner. It would be better to take more time finding the right partner than to act too quickly and select one that will turn out to be a problem down the road. If a potential partner is someone that you do not know at all, take time to get to know him. Go out to dinner, have discussions about your respective work histories, talk about each others' families. Remember, unlike hiring an employee, all questions are fair game when meeting with potential partners.

Fourth, meet with an attorney. There are many legal questions that will arise in a partnership discussion. These topics will include the type of business entity that is most appropriate for the kind of business you plan on starting, equity distribution, investment requirements, exit strategies, a buy-sell agreement, shareholders' agreement, and operating agreement. An attorney will act as an impartial intermediary and prepare all of the necessary legal documents. Select an attorney that specializes in business entities. You would not see an obstetrician if you have back pain. Similarly, select an attorney that is expert in the area in which you require service.

Fifth, assign areas of responsibility. The advantage to having two partners is that one person does not have to do all the work. Discuss the skills and experiences you each have and assign tasks and responsibilities to ensure that the best decisions are made in these areas each day.

Allow each other to make decisions. Do not try to control each other's actions. Do not micro-manage your partner. Agree on what types of decisions can be made individually and which ones require consensus.

Selecting the right partner will be your first major business decision. Make an educated decision using a thorough vetting process based on all of your needs. Do not make a hasty or emotional decision. Your partner will be with you until death, sale or insolvency do you part.

Chapter 8

Managing Money – Cash is King

As you read this book, you experience a writing style that is somewhat light, sometimes lighthearted, factual and serious but in a caring sort of way. This chapter is not written in that style. Do not read this chapter right after eating, it might get you upset. There is one element, one concept about running a business that is paramount above all else and that is "cash is king."

What is the most important element of a business? Is it sales, marketing, finance, operations, human resources, technology, gross profit or net profit? If you answered sales, marketing, finance, operations, human resources, technology, gross profit or net profit you are wrong. It is cash flow.

So what is cash flow and why is it so important? Cash flow is the movement of cash in and out of a business. It is that simple. Cash that comes in minus cash that goes out during a finite period of time (i.e., a month) is the cash flow. If more money comes in than goes out, then you have positive cash flow. That is good. If more money goes out than comes in, then you have negative cash flow. That is bad.

Cash flow is not the same as profit. Believe it or not, a company can show a profit and have negative cash flow; but I'm going to save that concept for the next book. So, if given the choice, would you want to own a company that had $1 million profit but $100,000 negative cash flow or a business that has $100,000 profit and $100,000 positive cash flow? (I hope you selected B. Now, under certain circumstances, "A" could be the better answer, but that explanation will also be in the second book.)

Now that we completely understand the value of cash flow and that everything you do should revolve around it, there are certain realities about running a business that you will have to accept, especially if things do not go as planned. In this chapter we will deal with the harsh realities of being an entrepreneur and making your business not only survive but be successful. Unfortunately, you may have to play the role of "bad guy" to achieve your goals, but this comes with the territory.

Let's start with a realistic scenario. Remember, to be an entrepreneur means no fear, so let's go through the process of identifying problems and finding solutions. Here is a business example:

"The economy slows down. Sales drop. Your customers begin to slow pay so your cash flow decreases dramatically. Your business is now running in the red (meaning it is showing a loss at the end of each month.) Key employees leave because they don't think your business will survive."

First question, true or false, the recession is causing my business to fail.
Answer: False. It is your fault!

The good news is that with smaller companies these problems are caused by internal occurrences not external ones like the economy. So, all you need to do is to look at your operation and determine what is wrong and fix it. So what are you going to do about this problem of running in the red? How will you turn things around?

Here comes the first dose of reality about being an entrepreneur. You must learn to make hard decisions. Your business comes first, because your business takes care of you and your family. If the world wants to play hardball, you have to play hardball or you will lose and that is not an acceptable outcome. Following are some actions that you may not be inclined to take because you have always wanted to be the boss that everybody loves. You are losing money! There is no time left for being nice, so you have to get your company back into the black or with positive cash flow immediately.

1. **If your business begins to fail during a recession or economic downturn, it is your fault**. Acknowledge that. It is time to take action. Do not go into ostrich mode by sticking your head in the sand and hoping that it goes away. By the time you take your head out of the sand, it will be time to close your business for good.

2. **You are not a victim**. In fact, no one cares about your predicament. If you were working 50 hours a week, you now need to work 70 hours a week. Whatever you need to do to turn things

around you must do because it is your responsibility.

3. **Throw teamwork out of the window.** Teamwork is overrated and it really doesn't work all that well in small businesses. If you rely on your team to turn things around you will actually be relying on your weakest link, and that weakest link will then inevitably bring down the entire operation. In times of crisis, employees want strong leadership and more structure. Focus on each individual's performance. Set higher and more difficult goals. Your employees need to know that at the end of the day they report to you, not to each other. Teamwork will lead to excuses, mediocrity and failure.

4. **It is time to micromanage.** As much as employees may not want this form of management, it will be necessary. If you delegate responsibility, make sure that the work is getting done correctly and on time. Never turn over the management of your business to someone else regardless of their experience. Begin asking for "flash" reports every day, if necessary, so you know exactly what is going on

at all times. Become a control freak and make sure that everyone is doing everything they are supposed to be doing every minute of every day.

5. **Freeze Salaries, no raises, no exceptions**. Especially in a small business, it is essential that you are paying employees for performance that translates to real profitability. Pay for performance means employees get paid for achieving specific objectives. Sales people should have 80% to 100% of their compensation based on performance. In fact, you should also be open to the idea of setting up systems within your company that actually penalizes employees for poor performance. This concept is so critical to running a small business that if you do not establish these kinds of policies as soon as you start your business the first person that should be fired is you.

6. **Motivate by fear**. Unfortunately, in small businesses being respected is not always enough to motivate employees. Sometimes it needs to be downright fear. This doesn't mean they should necessarily fear you as a person, but each employee should have a healthy fear that if the

business does not succeed that they will not be receiving a paycheck. In the end, although employees may not like a boss whom they fear, they will be thankful when the business is cash positive and they continue to be employed.

Well, wasn't that an interesting lesson in crisis management. These are the harsh realities of running a small business that does not have a high cash reserve and can easily weather economic storms. Are you sure you still want to be an entrepreneur?

Although profits and cash flow are not the same, you cannot have positive cash flow without profits. So, what exactly is "profit?" Profit is how much money is left over after you pay out all of your business's costs, which costs include the cost of the item you are selling (cost of goods), your sales and marketing expenses, and your general operating expenses.

A common mistake made by start-up companies is to confuse sales with making money. The best example of this can be with American automakers. General Motors may have sales of $20 billion in a given year but GM can lose $2 billion in that same year. Sales do not equate to profits on any scale.

Another common mistake is that profit is not taken into account for every sales transaction. Owners will promote big discounts in order to secure a sale without realizing that they may have actually lost money on those transactions. Effectively, in this scenario, the more you sell the more you lose, even though your sales are increasing. This is a very bad situation to get into and will ruin your business very quickly.

In order to create a profitable sale, you must understand the elements of your sale and the related business costs. Your sale price should be determined after all other elements are identified. Let's use an example.

If you wanted to sell a book, it is reasonable to say you think you should sell that book for $10. But, in reality, at this point in time, you have no idea whether or not you can make any money (profit) by selling that book for $10. You need to first know what it costs you to publish the book. Then how much money will it cost you to advertise the sale of the book, and other marketing tactics you may employ to sell your book, for example, through social networking sites, etc. If you are using a fulfillment house to package and mail the book, there are those costs. Then you must apply some amount of your general operating costs to that book. (General operating costs are your payroll, taxes, subscriptions, office supplies, postage, rent, travel & entertainment costs, etc.) Going through this exercise, you may find that you actually have $11 of cost per book; therefore your $10 price will lose you money on each transaction. You would then adjust your selling price to $15 or more.

Here are a few ideas about how to make a profit:

1. **About pricing**. Many new business owners believe they must offer the lowest price for their product or service in order to compete effectively with competitors. This will be a recipe for disaster. Why? Because if your value

proposition is about being the least expensive in the market, all a customer has to do is to find a lower price somewhere else and they will not buy from you. You do need to understand the market, your customers and your competitors when it comes to pricing; but your value proposition needs to be more than the price point. If you are selling widgets, you can rely on quality, on time delivery, customer service, ability to repair or replace, even your brand identity.

2. **Sell higher margin products and services.** You and your sales team need to have an intimate understanding of which items have the highest margins and try to steer customers in the direction of the higher margin items.

3. **Forget discounts.** Where do the dollars for a discount come from? Although you may think it is a reduction in sales (which it is) the discount dollars come from your profits. If you sell a $500 suit that normally has a 25% profit margin ($125) and you offer a discount of $100, you have given away 85% of your profit. If you have only 15% gross profit left after your sale, you

will most likely not cover your operating expenses and therefore lose money on that transaction. The better offer is to giveaway a $100 shirt with the purchase of that same suit. Why? Because your actual cost on that shirt may be only $50, thus, you have saved $50 on the overall transaction, the customer will perceive the same dollar value, and wind up with two items instead of one.

4. **Product mix, "smoduct" mix**. If you have a retail store that offers 100 different items for sale, and 10% are very slow movers with low margins, get them out of the product mix you offer to your customers. Sell those items off, get rid of them and sell the higher margin items.

If you decide to take the leap and become an entrepreneur, everything must be about positive cash flow first, and everything else a distant second. Second includes sales, marketing, human resources, operations, your products and services, technology, reporting, everything. **Without positive cash flow you have no business.**

Chapter 9

Sales – Lifeblood of Your Business

For everyone considering starting a business, there is one thing you will all have in common regardless of the type of business you decide to start. All of you will be required to sell either a product or a service to someone else. In this chapter, we will not try to overcomplicate the selling process. In fact, it is really rather simple if you follow some very basic tenets.

Customers are suspicious of salespeople and there is a good reason for this. Salespeople are trained to deal with closing a sale, efficient use of leads (the percentage of leads that converts to a sale), and overcoming objections. This approach is all about the salesperson and not about the customer. Put your customer first. Make the sale itself secondary to your customer's satisfaction.

This concept is so simple that it almost seems paradoxical. Stop trying to control your customers' behaviors and you will get better sales results than if you try every selling trick in the book. People want to buy from people they trust. The best way to become trustworthy is by putting the customers' interests first, by being sincere, honest and transparent and by offering a product or service that has value.

When customers trust you good things happen. They will continue to buy from you in the future. They will refer your company to others that will result in more sales. You will develop a great reputation. Customers will haggle less about price if they trust you and believe they are getting value from you, your product and your employees. Your trustworthiness will eventually be able to be used as a tactical marketing weapon against competitors.

Here are some mantras that I have used over the years to help develop relationships with customers. See if any of them ring true to you.

1. Do not try to control people if you want them to cooperate with you.

2. If you help someone or solve a problem your chances of making a sale increases.
3. If you listen to people first, they will listen to you.
4. You will get more sales by providing people what they need other than trying to sell them what you want.

So how do you prove to your customers that you can be trusted? Well, you must be believable, but not by simply saying you and your products are the best, but by conveying to them that there are good reasons or proof to believe you. There are three (3) basic kinds of proof you can offer to your customers:

1. **Facts**. Provide research that shows your product's value or greater popularity when compared to your competitors.

2. **Technical proof**. Provide evidence on the effectiveness of your product.

3. **Testimonials**. Comments or letters from your customers supporting your products, services and company as a whole.

Most important is that when you do offer proof of any kind that it is believable to your customers. Believability can be achieved by offering proof from credible sources.

The Value Proposition

The single most important element in the selling process is the Value Proposition. The value proposition is a description of the customer's problem, the solution that addresses the problem, and the value of this solution from the customer's perspective. You should be able to present your value proposition in 30 seconds or less, or if in print, through the use of 3 to 5 bullet points or short phrases. A value proposition should also be presented from the customer's perspective, not from your company's perspective. Following is an example of a common value proposition used in many sales pitches regarding the company's shipping policies. The first is from the company's perspective, the second from the customer's perspective.

Company's perspective: "We ship in 3 to 5 business days."

Customer's perspective: "Your order will arrive at your home in 3 to 5 days."

A value proposition usually contains five essential elements:

- Image
- Features
- Advantages
- Benefits
- Offer

The *image* refers to a photograph, drawing, picture or diagram of the product. People tend to remember pictures easier than words.

The *features* are those elements of your product that may be unique.

The *advantages* are those features that set your product apart from those of your competitor.

The *benefits* define how you solve a customer's problem.

The *offer* is the specific call to action. Let your customers know how and when to buy by using expressions like, "limited time offer" or by offering a telephone number to call. When composing and offer, remember these four important elements:

1. **Keep it clear**. Do not make it difficult for your customers to figure out what the offer is.

2. **Keep it simple**. Keep your offer statement simple so it is easy to understand.

3. **Keep it brief**. Use as few words as possible.

4. **Keep it immediate**. You want them to buy now not a month from now.

The key to sales is giving the customer more than what they are paying for it. Every purchase by a customer is considered an investment, so each customer will measure their purchase in terms of their return on their investment. You want your customers to perceive the greatest possible value from your product or service so that they feel they are getting far more than what they paid. If not, they would then believe they are getting a "negative return on investment" that will result in a dissatisfied customer, a loss of your credibility, and the likelihood that your customer will make his next purchase from a competitor.

As you will read in the next chapter, a satisfied customer is not only a source of future sales but also becomes part of your marketing strategy. Satisfied customers will tell others about your products, your company and even about you making your future marketing a whole lot easier.

Chapter 10

Marketing - Success Depends on It

Many people confuse the functions of sales and marketing thinking they are basically the same thing. They are not, so let's start with very simple definition of marketing.

"Marketing" is the promotion of your business, product and services. Marketing is letting the world know that your company and your products exist, how and where your products can be purchased, pricing, its functions, its benefits, and so on.

Unlike the other areas of a business, there are many functions within the marketing area and there are also many different kinds of marketing. In this chapter, we will provide a brief explanation of each one. All or most of these functions will also become elements of a marketing plan that will help you to plan and track your marketing programs.

The larger the enterprise the more complex and detailed a marketing plan should be. Do not let the scope of a marketing plan intimidate you. Most small, start-up businesses do not need a plan with a high level of complexity, but it is good to know you have options particularly if you will be seeking investor money. It is possible a well-defined marketing plan may be a condition of an investment, so it is better to be prepared. In the Appendix is a complete marketing plan, but in this chapter we will discuss only those elements needed to get your business up and running.

How to Create a Marketing Plan

A marketing plan will play an important role in the success of your new business. A carefully-devised plan is the key to marketing success because it focuses your attention on the goals that will bring you success, as well as helps you pinpoint the best route for achieving those goals. Business conditions can evolve and change from month to month, but a well-crafted plan will roll with the changes.

In general, you can follow these 7 steps to create your marketing plan. Following this outline are some more detailed definitions of these key elements.

Step 1: Assess your products or services
Analyze the marketability of your product or service. Is there something special about it that will appeal to your target customers? Is it unique? Well designed? Priced correctly? Consider all possibilities for angles you could use to market your products or services.

Step 2: Do market research
Learn about your customers, your competitors and your industry. Examine the strengths and weaknesses of your company and those of your competitors. Study industry trends. Do as much research as necessary to help you fully understand your market so that you can generate the interest that will lead to the sales that will boost the profits.

Step 3: Establish objectives
Set goals.

Step 4: Create a budget
Determine how much money will be required to achieve your goals. Do not spread yourself too thin by implementing many different plans at the same time. Stick to those tactics that will reach the greatest number of your target customers.

Step 5: Draft your plan
Your marketing plan will include the strategies, tactics that you will use, the objectives you want to achieve and how much money it will cost.

Step 6: Track results
Tracking the results of your efforts is necessary to making sure that you get what you pay for and that you're moving toward success. If the results show that you are having issues with certain segments of your plan, then you will need to adjust and make changes. A marketing plan is a dynamic tool and may require modifications from time to time to maximize the use of your marketing dollars.

Below are the elements of a marketing plan that most start-up businesses should consider developing:

Executive Summary

Having an understanding of your industry, competitors and customers will be one of the keys to your success. In the Situation Analysis section, understand these elements and reduce them to writing, even if done without a great amount of detail. Show that you understand the elements of your business.

The Executive Summary is a synopsis of the entire marketing plan. Since some investors only read this section to determine whether they should spend more time evaluating your plan (and company), it should highlight the main elements of your plan and business strategy, and create a desire to read the rest of the document.

Briefly summarize the following:
- Current Situation, Company Mission & Objectives
- Product/Service Description
- Marketing Objectives
- Major Marketing Programs & Strategy
- Expected Marketing and/or Financial Results
- Keys to Success

The sections above should contain answers to the following questions:

- **Who?** (Who is your company? Who are the target customers?)
- **What?** (What is the product or service offered?)
- **Where?** (Where is your market located? Where will you be implementing your marketing activities?)
- **When?** (When will your plan be implemented? When do you expect the results?)
- **How much?** (How much sales, cost, profits, and ROI do you expect?)

5 Ways to Murder Your Marketing Plan

A good marketing plan is like a game plan. It is a tactical guide to help your business grow. A marketing plan needs to have flexibility in case you need to shift strategies from time to time or to gain new market share. However, a good plan does not need to be long and complicated.

A good marketing plan employs sound strategies and tactics. Of all of the elements that can be contained in a plan, those that relate to the more "creative" elements such as branding, although important, are not as vital as beginning your plan with an understanding of the basics, which ironically is less about marketing and more about accounting. With that said, here are five common mistakes you should avoid:

1. "Fluff" is not "stuff". There are three components of a marketing plan: a) strategies; b) tactics; and c) the numbers. Whatever your product or service is going to be, do not believe that "everyone" is your market. Determine who your perfect customers are and develop a plan around how to acquire and retain them. For example, do not define "all women over 25" as your market. Get more specific. Reduce it down to "women between the ages of 25 and 50 who shop in brick-and-mortar stores with average incomes greater than $40,000 per year." When you go to a store, you do not buy everything in it. The same is true for marketing to potential customers. As much as you may want to purchase everything in a store, you have limited resources, so employ the same approach when marketing. It must be targeted and limited to the amount of money you have to market to that customer niche. Come up with a plan and stick to it.

2. Marketing is about Math. As much as this may sound like a contradiction, marketing is less about creativity and more about managing money and data results. To be successful, you must understand your costs, sales, profits, and the lifetime value of each customer. If you spend $1,000 on an advertisement, how many leads and sales you will need to recover your cost and to make a profit.

3. Creativity vs. Success. There is certainly a place for creativity but do not trade creativity for sound tactics. Highly creative marketing techniques and brand strategies may not necessarily result in sales. Be creative but know your numbers. This is what will ultimately drive your business to success.

4. Marketing is not only Advertising. When thinking about marketing, think broadly and understand that it is not only about advertising your product or service. Advertising is one aspect of marketing, but as you read in this chapter, marketing is made up of many elements including understanding your market and customers, doing analysis work, pricing strategies, sales strategies, promotions, your competitive edge, brand development, your logo, website, online sales capabilities, and of course, the ability to capture and understand data to ensure a proper return on investment.

5. Don't forget to market to Existing Customers. The fastest way to grow your business quickly is to retain and market to your existing customers. It can cost up to six times as much to acquire a new customer than to get an existing customer to make a new purchase. Your existing customers have the greatest potential for recurring sales with less cost associated to each one.

Getting the Biggest Bang for Your Buck – How to Manage Advertising Dollars

With the recent slowdown in the U.S. economy, most segments are considered "buyers' markets." This is particularly true in advertising, which is good news if you are starting a new business or planning on spending additional dollars to launch revised marketing strategies. In fact, compared to just a few short years ago, smaller advertisers were routinely bumped from print, radio and TV ads in favor of larger advertisers or they were getting stuck on waiting lists for outdoor billboards in high traffic areas.

So, when developing an advertising budget, make sure you are going to get the biggest bang for your buck by remembering a few simple things:

1. **Don't be afraid to negotiate**. If you don't ask, you don't get. In today's market, when you purchase advertising, ask about additional mentions on TV spots, co-sponsorships on promotions, bigger ads or better placements for print ads, or more frequency on radio spots for the same dollars.

2. **Leads are better than branding**. Especially for a company in start-up mode, generating leads (and sales) is more important than building your brand (despite what ad agency people will tell you.) When buying advertising, do it with a focus on lead generation and not on brand building. Make sure the ads you do run have a "call to action."

3. **Don't forget public relations**. You are starting a new business in a down economy. You are bucking the trend and therefore should have a newsworthy story to be told by the media. Position you and your company as being a contrarian, going against the trend, optimistic about the future where others are pessimistic. Try to use your own story as a point of light for the media to pick up on. The public's perception of you, your company and your products will be remembered for many years to come.

4. Direct mail versus email marketing. Explore whether or not direct mail makes sense for your type of business. Although the trend right now is to spend money on email marketing, the reality is that the average click-through rates are less than half of one percent, and a click-through does not necessarily convert into a sale. Direct mail conversion rates average 1 to 2 percent when using a general mailing list; however, a list specifically designed to be sent to your target customer base with a very specific call to action can result in response rates considerably higher.

I will restate a theme running through this chapter: track your costs, response rates, sales and profits. The more you know about how your customers respond to your advertising tactics the more likely you are to increase your rate of return on the dollars you spend.

Focus on Your Core Customers

We mentioned earlier how important it is to market to your existing customers, but even more important, to retain them. The cost of acquiring a new customer can be as high as six times that as maintaining an existing customer. Do not take your customers for granted at the expense of trying to secure new ones.

For your business to survive and grow understand these two concepts:

1. Your best opportunity for acquiring new customers is through your core customers

2. Your business's single greatest risk is the loss of core customers

A "core" customer is one who repeatedly purchases from you, is dedicated to your product offering and is willing to promote your business to potential new customers. Following are some simple steps to remember about how to manage core customers:

1. Understand who your customers are. Everyone is not a core customer.

2. Are your customers satisfied? If a customer is not satisfied they will simply buy what they need from a competitor, and most likely, never tell you why they left. Ask and listen to their problems, your mistakes and why they may not be happy. Do everything you can to retain these customers by resolving problems.

3. Be proactive and communicate with your core customers. Let your customers know you care about them and their success. Resolve problems. Accept feedback and react to their concerns. Do everything you can keep them happy.

4. Talk is cheap... deliver! All businesses talk the talk; make sure you walk the walk. Of course each business will tell customers they are important and that the "customer always come first" but all do not practice what they preach. Show them you care. When you deliver what you promise, your customers will remember, and in turn, let others know about how they are treated.

5. Understand their needs and become invaluable. In today's economy, simply being a product or service provider is not be enough. Many customers will evaluate their relationship with you and your business following each purchase. So, find ways to become an invaluable asset to your customers not just a supplier. By communicating, you may find that there is a demand for ancillary products or services. If you can fulfill this demand, you are providing greater value to your customers, thus becoming a much more valuable asset to them.

Building a Million Dollar Brand without a lot of Money

It is a myth to believe that in order to build a brand you must spend a great deal of money. It is true that companies do fail because of a lack of funding that needs to be dedicated to brand building, but you don't need to spend a fortune to develop a brand and build your business. Start close to home and invest your money in branding techniques that will expose your company to the greatest number of potential customers in the shortest amount of time.

Customers need to believe that you are able to play with the big boys. This can be done by investing your money and positioning your company so it is perceived that your business is impressive, motivational and inspirational without breaking your bank.

1. Your Website. In today's world, your website will become the center of the local, regional, national and international markets. You want to build a website that is clean, easy to navigate, contains useful content and makes your company look far more established than it may actually be. Design your site with the needs of your customers in mind. Don't worry if you do not know how to build a website. There are many services out there that can do this for you at a relatively low cost.

2. Choose the right Domain Name. Also referred to as a URL (Uniform Resource Locator), your URL can be a vital element in your brand strategy. Try to keep your URL to 10 letters or less. Make it easy to remember. Avoid the use of dashes in your URL or other forms of punctuation. Create a URL with the "*.com" extension and stay away from .net or .tv if you can.

3. Vanity Telephone Numbers. Vanity numbers may not be applicable for all business, but for products or services being sold directly to consumers, vanity numbers become an easier way for customers to remember your business's phone number and statistically it has been shown that inbound phone calls increase significantly when an easy to remember vanity number is available to customers.

4. Your Business Address. Again, depending on the nature of your business, if for example, your business provides a service to other businesses, it can be important for your customers to believe they are calling your company's global headquarters even if you are running your business out of your den. For relatively small amounts of money, you can rent a virtual office to secure an impressive address.

5. Your Logo. Create a logo for your business that is memorable, but one that looks professional. Do not use a lot of colors that clash or complicated designs. Have it be clean and quickly identifiable.

6. Your Business Card. Once you have your logo, domain name, address and telephone number, create a business card that looks professional. Your business card will make the initial impression about your company. A cheap, uninspired business card could possibly send the wrong message to a perspective customer. Use a thicker card stock and a high quality finish. Sometimes even a different shape or size can work better than the traditional business card. Regardless, the message you want to send with your card is one of professionalism and high quality.

As you can see, there are many elements to marketing. Marketing includes advertising, branding, public relations, promotions, knowing your industry, competitors and customers, pricing, budgeting, and most important, accumulating and analyzing data. Remember, it is not about how much you spend, but how wisely you spend it. Marketing is about creating a successful return on your investment first and building your brand a distant second.

Story time: *Sometimes the best way to explain a concept is with an example. This is a true case study involving the landscaping company with which I contract that provides weekly lawn mowing services and other landscaping services on an as-needed basis. Jim has been the proud owner of his own landscaping company for over 20 years. This example will illustrate why Jim's business has survived and flourished for all these years, why he continues to expand his customer base, and why his existing customers don't switch to other landscaping providers.*

Spring 2009 arrived and I begin to receive flyer after flyer inserted into my front door or on the side of my mailbox advertising a variety of landscaping company options. So many from which to chose, but which ones are reliable? Offer the best prices and the best services? I decide to call one based on the location to my house. Unfortunately, they do not service my neighborhood but they are quick to refer my call to Jim's company and telling me how great he is. Well, that referral and endorsement certainly went a long way, so I gave Jim a call.

The next Saturday there is a knock on my door. It is Jim introducing himself and his company to me personally and letting me know that he would love to work for me, that he offers fair prices and that he has a great team of guys that will make the house look great and keep it looking great all summer. Without me asking my questions, Jim already answered most of them, so I agreed to give him a chance. Seeing that he now had me as a new customer and having worked out the weekly fee for lawn mowing services, Jim quickly began making suggestions about how to make the property look better in a very professional, but unobtrusive way. (He was up-selling me!)

Jim suggested that a full yard clean-up be done as soon as possible that would include the trimming of bushes and trees, edging the walkway areas, weeding all of the flower beds, and mulching. I agreed with Jim's suggestions and wound up spending $500 for work that probably would have taken me two weeks to do myself.

Jim promises that my lawn mowing day will be every Thursday unless there are weather problems that would not allow his team to do their work. Sure enough, when Thursday came, so did Jim's crew. 20 minutes later, the property looked great and they were on their way. This continued throughout the summer.

Jim picked up two new customers in our neighborhood because of the great work that he was doing on my property simply because of the quality of the work. Residents who walk the neighborhood saw the quality of his work, his trucks with the company name prominently displayed on the side, along with his phone number. They called.

Every few weeks Jim would personally stop by and ask how his guys were doing and if I was satisfied or if there was anything else that they could do for me. He also shared that he picked up new business in the area and thanked me even though I had nothing to do with it really.

So 2009 comes and goes. 2010 arrives and there is that same knock at the door. Jim returning to see if I would like him to provide services to me again this spring and summer. No impersonal flyers stuck in my door or a note sent to me in the mail assuming I would contract with his company. He wanted to make sure that I would contract again and it was worth a personal trip to my house. While we are talking about the upcoming season, out of his wallet comes pictures of his new baby girl that was just born. Jim has chosen to now make the business relationship more personal.

It was only seconds after the wallet was put away that Jim began to ask me about the yard clean-up for 2010, looking around, making all sorts of suggestions to make the property look great for the new spring/summer season. $1,500 later, my property was the talk of the neighborhood. But, there was a problem! While edging one of the flower beds, one of Jim's guys accidentally cut the cable wire coming into my house. I had no TV, phone or computer services! I called the cable company to set up a service call, but it was going to be 5 days before they could come out.

Later that afternoon Jim came by to see how the project was going. We walked the property together inspecting and I had to let Jim know that one of his guys accidentally cut my cable line. He felt terrible, but it was an accident. I told him I would be without services for 5 days. Jim told me he had an employee who dealt with his electrical needs and that he would call him. One hour later, a man pulled up to my house with his family in the car, got out, and repaired the cable line. Everything worked fine. I thanked him and he left.

I asked Jim about his employee that came to fix the cable wire. Jim was honest and told me that it was his day off and that was why his family was in the car. Even though his man was at my house for about 15 minutes, Jim told me he paid him for two hours of work to thank him for coming out on his day off. I then got the story about how Jim takes care of all of his employees and how many of them have been working for him for years.

But the story does not end there. Two weeks after Jim's team completed the yard clean-up, I get a phone call. Jim knew I liked to play golf, so he told me that he was putting together a foursome to go and play at a nearby resort course, and that he was picking up the tab! He was taking out three of his best customers for a round of golf. How could I refuse (I never refuse golf.) Two weeks later, I was meeting two of Jim's customers and we were teeing off for a day of golf.

His team continues to show up every Thursday as

promised. Every few weeks Jim calls to make sure his guys are doing a great job and to see if I am happy with his services. He also asks me if there is anything else that I might need from him.

Jim's landscaping business is the quintessential example of marketing a business. Jim understands the marketplace and that there is a lot of competition. He knows he must differentiate himself somehow from the competition to get an edge. Jim chooses to employ the personal contact method (which obviously worked in my case.) His pricing is fair and competitive. Jim, although the owner with dozens of customers, takes the time to personally stay in touch with me always wanting to know if his "guys" are doing a great job. Believe me, if there was a problem it would be fixed in a minute. Jim would consider me a "core" customer, so he makes an extra effort to market to me (extra phone calls, baby pictures, and golf). Jim clearly takes care of his employees as well. He has a big summer party at his house for his workers and their families, pays them fairly and works with them hand in hand on major projects.

Jim's business has grown over the years not by mistake or luck but by design by following many of the marketing principles outlined in this chapter. Jim's business is a small, local business that employs marketing strategies that work and without spending large amounts of money. Jim knows his industry, the market, his competitors, pricing, customer relations, problem resolution, and especially customer retention!

Chapter 11

Building Your Team

You are almost ready to start your business. You have your product or service defined. You created a business plan and a marketing plan. You raised some start-up capital and created a budget. You selected a name, incorporated your business, and created a website. Just before you open for business, depending on the type of business you are starting, you may need to hire employees.

Even the best entrepreneurs that have had successful careers in corporate America do not know or can successfully run all of the functional areas of a company. No one is good at everything, and if you believe that you will be starting your business with a clear disadvantage. So, it might be necessary to hire people to help you run your business. *Hire people with skills that can help you expand your business!*

When hiring people, follow a few simple steps that will pay big dividends down the road:

1. **Define the work you need done, not the position you want to hire.**

Define your company's challenges and the outcomes you expect then look for someone with the skills and experience to solve those challenges. Do not do it the other way around.

2. **Challenge the norm.**

Do not get caught in the trap of hiring people because this is the way it is done. Look for people with similar values and work ethic but that may have varying perspectives. When interviewing, present your challenges to them to see how they would solve the problem. You might be surprised to hear of new ways to solve certain problems that you haven't thought of yet.

3. **Do not hire yourself.**

Do not try to hire a replica of yourself. Acknowledge that people are different and that they have different ideas and ways of doing things. These people will offer different perspectives on business challenges; however, you do want to hire people with whom you are philosophically aligned.

4. **Know what to expect from your new employee.**

Write a clear, well-defined job description including goals. When you interview, you will be able to articulate the position and both employer and applicant will have the opportunity to determine if the position is a good fit for both parties.

5. **Know what kind of boss you are and what you expect.**

Do you want employees that are independent thinkers or someone that checks in often? Do you believe in providing a lot of verbal and written reinforcement or do you expect people to just get the job done? When you interview, find out what makes for a productive work environment for both you and your new employee, and make sure they jive. If they don't, you may wind up with two very unhappy people.

6. **Use a reputable company that provides background checks.**

If you are starting a business where you will have employees working in "high value areas" such as handling a lot of money or inventory, or your business deals with accessing customers' homes, or working with children, you may want to have background checks done before you make the decision to hire. This has become a very common practice among all size businesses.

7. Seek referrals.

Go out into the marketplace and find referrals for good candidates. People that can provide personal experiences from past work relationships with new applicants can be invaluable in your decision making process.

8. Develop a well-defined training program.

Nothing is more frustrating to a new employee than coming into a new job and no one is there to show you how to do it properly. A training program should cover all aspects of the job, especially the expectations of the company. A training program can be a one-on-one training for a predetermined amount of time or a detailed manual. It will be up to you to determine which one will work most successfully in your new business environment.

A Company's Secret Weapon: Training

Being completely honest, training is one of those areas within a business that is perceived as being boring, tedious and marginally necessary. Entrepreneurs and business leaders want to focus on the more glamorous and results-oriented areas of finance, cash management, and new business development. Don't make this mistake.

Let's take a look at six common misconceptions about training:

Misconception #1: **If you hire quality people and pay them a lot of money you don't really need to train them, they will figure it out.**

Fact: This could hold to be true in a very small business with only one or two employees. The reality is as your business grows, the boss becomes more detached from his employees and from the day-to-day operations. Customers are far too expensive to acquire and retain and they cannot be left to be managed by new hires that will guess at how to best handle them.

Misconception #2: **If you spend a lot of time and money training on an employee they will simply take that knowledge and leave.**

Fact: It has been proven that solid training programs are actually a retention tool. The reasons people leave companies have very little to do with training and more to do with the culture, pay scales, advancement opportunities, and the like.

Misconception #3: Training costs too much.

Fact: Taxes cost too much, not training. Paying taxes has no direct benefit to a company. It is an expense with no measurable return. Conversely, training will immediately make contributions to your company in the form of fewer errors, higher productivity, improved sales and better customer relations.

Misconception #4: You will implement training programs when things slow down a bit or when you have more money to invest.

Fact: No you won't. That is an excuse because you simply do not understand the value of training. Understand that good training will improve your business almost immediately, and improved business means more profit.

Misconception #5: On-the-job training is the best kind of training.

Fact: Well, this is kind of a trick question. The answer is, it might be, but also may not be. It really depends on the nature of your business. There is certainly value in on-the-job training, but sometimes classroom training, even done by an outside provider, sometimes speeds up the learning curve. A great example is payroll processing. When I personally had occasion to learn our company's payroll function there were certainly people capable of training me, but one 8-hour session at ADP gave me more technical knowledge and continuity than I could have possibly received on the job.

Misconception #6: Mentoring is better than training.

Fact: No it isn't. Mentoring is a second rate variation of on-the-job training where you take the new guy and attach him to the hip of the old guy and tell him to do what he does. That is the "monkey see, money do" approach to learning a business. Unless you are running a zoo, this is no way to run a business. The new guy will only see the functions without really learning the nuances or reasons behind what he is doing. Trust me on this one; the Old Guy is not going to explain nuances to the New Guy. First of all, he doesn't know what nuances are, and second of all, he thinks the New Guy is there to take his job. Don't expect much from this approach. There is no incentive to teach or to learn.

Training will improve your company's productivity and develop happier employees, not to mention the added profits it will contribute to your bottom line. Make training your secret weapon. Your competitors will not know what hit them.

Chapter 12

A Little Technology Goes a Long Way

Today's very competitive business climate demands that business owners understand and use advanced technologies. Technology can help a business improve efficiencies and even expand operations. However, the use of technology should be balanced with business needs and practicality.

Depending on the type of company you are starting, the role of technology will vary. When starting a business, you want to keep your costs to a minimum until you can start to get some sales traction and have a better idea on your cash flow. However, there will be some software and hardware that you will most likely require to handle some of your company's basic functions. Luckily, with the growth of entrepreneurial businesses in America, many of the basic softwares are fairly simple to use and does not require a high level of technology of expertise.

Most companies, even start-ups, will need some type of accounting software. In the Appendix section there is a list comparing the more popular accounting software packages available in the marketplace. The Appendix is titled, "*2010 Accounting Software Review Product Comparisons*." QuickBooks even offers a free version to handle the very basic functions, but that works just fine especially when starting up.

Technology runs a fairly large gamut encompassing telephone systems, Internet connections, websites, cell phones, laptops, desktops, server-based systems, back-up systems, and an endless list of software to consider. Again, depending on the nature of your business, you will have to decide if you need a word processing software (i.e. Microsoft Word), spreadsheets (i.e., Excel), databases, publishing, mail systems, online order entry systems, and so on. If you are not techno savvy, find a friend, relative or even hire a consultant who can make recommendations on what types of hardware and software you might need to effectively run your business.

Technology can be an expensive proposition not only to purchase but to maintain. Start with the basics, the things you absolutely need to start and run your business, and to properly communicate with your customers. There are even free software packages out there, some of which are listed below. These can help you to minimize your technology expenses when you are launching your new business.

Making VoIP Calls: SKYPE

The latest version of Skype offers better audio quality while using 50 percent less bandwidth. The improved video calls are now easier to start and can fill up your whole screen at a 30 frames per second. A new screen-sharing feature allows you to share a document, presentation, or website with another Skype user. Skype charges for some features, but calls to other Skype users are always free.

Basic Accounting: QUICBOOKS SIMPLE START FEE EDITION

The free version of QuickBooks lets you create invoices, print checks, handle payroll, and manage up to 20 customer accounts. There are plenty of free bookkeeping tools on the market, but QuickBooks is the best option for startup and growing companies. QuickBooks is easy to step up and to work within the various accounting functions. When you are ready to step up to the paid version (about $100), QuickBooks will allow you to track and report on up to 10,000 customers. (That should keep you busy for a while).

Syncing with Outlook: Google Calendar Sync

Many businesses are switching to Google Apps because it's cheaper than Microsoft Exchange. But not everyone wants to abandon the familiar look and feel of Outlook. Use this tool to sync from Google Calendar to Outlook or vice versa. You can even perform a two-way sync based on a schedule you set. Unfortunately, some of Google's features -- like e-mail reminders -- won't work in Outlook.

Technology is a subject that encompasses so much information that it is difficult to summarize everything that is available in the marketplace, especially for those of you looking to start a new business. Businesses vary greatly from product to product, service to service, how you sell, who your customers are, where your customers are, if you sell directly to consumers or to businesses. Just remember, when starting a business, keep your costs to a minimum. Do not be afraid of technology, embrace it. There are wonderful tools out there to help manage and grow your business. If you are not techno-savvy, find help. You will be the winner in the long run.

Chapter 13

Exit Strategies

Entrepreneurs tend to focus solely on starting their businesses by finding the product or service they will sell, putting together a business plan and a marketing plan, hiring people, identifying customers, and so on. But one element that is rarely considered when starting a business is how and when you will get out of the business. Planning on how you will end your relationship with your business is called an Exit Strategy.

It may be your intention to invest your time and money into a venture that you intend to pass on to your children. This is certainly one kind of exit strategy because it still involves you leaving the business at some point. But even for a legacy company, you need to plan on how you will exit the company. Who will run it? How will you get your investment out of the company.

Without consideration for a legacy transaction or an IPO (initial public offering, taking the company public), there are four (4) very basis kinds of exit strategies. If you are going to "pull the trigger" and start a business, discuss these possible exit strategies with your spouse and business partners, especially your business partners. You may find that partners have very different approaches on how to run and exit a business, so to avoid confusion, arguments and lawsuits, discuss, plan and document your exit strategy in advance.

Exit Strategy #1:   The Lifestyle Company – "Bleed It Dry"

A lifestyle company strategy works best if you do not have passive investors. This strategy involves pulling out as much money as possible from your company with little or no consideration for its future. This approach does not suggest running your company in the "red" or at a loss to accommodate your goals. The strategy involves paying to yourself the largest possible salary, a year-end bonus regardless of the company's annual performance, having the company pay for your car, purchasing insurance policies with company money to benefit you and your family in the long term, hiring family members, paying yourself very high interest rates for money you may loan to the company, and so on.

Although this practice would not be acceptable in a public company, it is common practice in private ones, especially smaller, single-owner companies. This strategy also does not necessarily involve growing the business larger and larger. Once you hit a targeted revenue and profit level, you keep the company at that size because you are withdrawing enough money each year to accommodate your chosen lifestyle.

In one anecdotal story from the Harvard Business School, a student asked the guest speaker who was also a small business owner why he would not grow his business bigger and then sell it for hundreds of millions of dollars. The owner's response was quite compelling and exemplifies this particular exit strategy. His response was, "Excuse me. What part of a 30 hour work week and income of $5 million a year of personal income do you not understand?"

Of course, with any strategy there are pros and cons.

Pros:
- Your take home pay is as high as you can make it
- You have no need to dedicate any of your time to future business planning

Cons:
- High income can have very serious tax implications each year
- If your business suffers a downturn, it will not have cash available to deal with the crisis

Exit Strategy #2: Liquidation

Liquidation is the simplest of all of the exit strategies. You simply decide when you have had enough and you call it quits, you close the business. Most entrepreneurs do not start a new business planning to liquidate it, but it happens all the time. Imagine if you are able to withdraw $5 million per year from your company for 10 years. This may allow you to have saved $30 million dollars (depending on your lifestyle and investment practices.) You turn 60 years old and do not want to go through the process of selling the company, you simply want to retire. You are wealthy and just want the work process to end, so you decide to end the business. It's that simple. You would sell all of the company's assets, pay your creditors and employees what they are due, and close the doors.

Pros:
- It is easy
- There is no need to spend time looking for a buyer. No negotiating.

- No issues about transfer of control

Cons:

- You will be leaving a lot of money on the table by not selling it to an interested buyer. You could walk away from a great deal of money for the sake of convenience.
- If you have other shareholders, they will be upset about this tactic.
- Your company's assets have value, for example, your customer list, business name, goodwill, and business relationships could also be sold separately.

Exit Strategy #3: Sell the Business to Family, Friend or Friendly Buyer

Different than an Acquisition that will be discussed as Exit Strategy #4; this strategy involves selling your business to a family member (children), a friend, a customer, your employees or some other friendly buyer. You may find that there are people who have become emotionally attached to your business or believe in the legacy value of the business and want to keep it alive. If the business is successful and has a fair number of employees, this may become an excellent opportunity for the employees to not only retain their jobs but to now become entrepreneurs themselves.

Pros:
- If your management and/or employees buy the business, they have a vested interest in making it work
- There is less due diligence involved if you know the buyer
- If the buyer has an emotional attachment to the business in some way, he/she will more likely maintain the company's integrity in the marketplace

Cons:
- Selling to family members can lead to fighting and arguments about how to manage the business going forward
- Selling to a family member or close friend may have you accept a low purchase price because you "like them"
- If the form of the sale is a stock sale (versus an asset sale), the new owner may find himself with unexpected liabilities to pay

Exit Strategy #4: Acquisition

Unlike selling your business to a family member or friend, in an acquisition you sell your company to another company. Here, there is one huge advantage: if you have run a successful business you can determine the selling price. Although there are the public markets that will estimate the value of your business, the sky is really the limit on what you perceive your company to be worth. Choosing the right company to acquire your company is the key. There must be a good fit, and if there is, it is not uncommon for the acquiring company to pay far more than the estimated market value of your company.

Pros:
- You determine the value of your company, not the public markets
- If you can get multiple companies to have an interest in buying your company, it could create a bidding war that will increase the selling price

Cons:
- If you manipulate your company operations to "fit" with a specific acquirer, you may limit your number of potential buyers
- If you have a genuine interest in your employees, combining cultures can often be difficult often leading to the termination of employees from the company being acquired
- The terms of an acquisition may constrain your personal lifestyle with non-compete, non-disclosure agreements

In conclusion, we tried to have one major recurring theme throughout this book and that is to plan. Plan before you even start a business and make sure you select a good product or service that you know you can sell and that there are customers that will buy. Plan your business with a solid business plan, marketing plan, budget, and cash management plan and have it be flexible enough to allow plans to change as your business changes. And last, but certainly not least, plan your exit strategy. The day will come when it is time to stop running your business. You may want to retire or simply sell your business. Regardless of your motivation, plan your exit strategy to maximize your return on investment. Remember, your investment will not have been only money but many years of hard work. You deserve the most successful end to a successful business run.

So, to all of you considering taking the big step and becoming an entrepreneur, remember the words of Gordon Gecko, entrepreneur and corporate raider from the movie, <u>Wall Street</u> (played by Michael Douglas.) When Gordon Gecko had the chance to speak at an annual shareholders' meeting he made it perfectly clear to all of the shareholders that "Greed is good." It is what motivates Americans and especially entrepreneurs. Do not be afraid to be successful and to become rich. Do not be afraid to try. It is the American way. Be honest with your customers, be fair, work hard, and succeed.

Appendix

APPENDIX I
PERSONAL STRENGTHS AND WEAKNESSES WORKSHEET

The chart below will help you identify your strengths and weaknesses and will give you a better idea if you're ready to become a small business owner. Examine each of the skills areas listed in the chart. Ask yourself whether you possess some or all of the skills listed in the parentheses. Then rate your skills in each area by circling the appropriate number, using a scale of 1-5, with 1 as low, 2 as between low and medium, 3 as medium, 4 as between medium and high, and 5 as high.

Skills	low	medium			high
Sales					
Pricing	1	2	3	4	5
Buying	1	2	3	4	5
Sales planning	1	2	3	4	5
Negotiating	1	2	3	4	5
Direct selling to buyers	1	2	3	4	5
Customer service follow-up	1	2	3	4	5
Managing other sales reps	1	2	3	4	5
Tracking competitors	1	2	3	4	5
Marketing					
Advertising/promotion/public relations	1	2	3	4	5
Annual marketing plans	1	2	3	4	5
Media planning and buying	1	2	3	4	5
Advertising copy writing	1	2	3	4	5
Marketing strategies	1	2	3	4	5
Distribution channel planning	1	2	3	4	5
Pricing	1	2	3	4	5
Packaging	1	2	3	4	5

Financial planning

Cash flow planning	1	2	3	4	5
Monthly financial	1	2	3	4	5
Bank relationships	1	2	3	4	5
Management of credit lines	1	2	3	4	5

Accounting

Bookkeeping	1	2	3	4	5
Billing, payables, receivables	1	2	3	4	5
Monthly profit and loss statements/balance sheets	1	2	3	4	5
Quarterly/annual tax preparation	1	2	3	4	5

Administrative

Scheduling	1	2	3	4	5
Payroll handling	1	2	3	4	5
Benefits administration	1	2	3	4	5

Personnel management

Hiring employees	1	2	3	4	5
Firing employees	1	2	3	4	5
Motivating employees	1	2	3	4	5
General management skills	1	2	3	4	5

Personal business skills

Oral presentation skills	1	2	3	4	5
Written communication skills	1	2	3	4	5
Computer skills	1	2	3	4	5
Word processing skills	1	2	3	4	5
Fax, email experience	1	2	3	4	5
Organizational skills	1	2	3	4	5

Intangibles					
Ability to work long and hard	1	2	3	4	5
Ability to manage risk and stress	1	2	3	4	5
Family support	1	2	3	4	5
Ability to deal with failure	1	2	3	4	5
Ability to work alone	1	2	3	4	5
Ability to work with and manage others	1	2	3	4	5
Total					

After you've rated yourself in each area, total up the numbers. Then apply the following rating scale:

- ❏ If your total is less than 20 points, you should reconsider whether owning a business is the right step for you.

- ❏ If your total is between 20 and 25, you're on the verge of being ready, but you may be wise to spend some time strengthening some of your weaker areas.

- ❏ If your total is above 25, you're ready to start a new business now.

APPENDIX II
START-UP COSTS WORKSHEET

This worksheet will help you to determine start-up costs associated with your new business. Complete this worksheet and transfer the total in the Financial Projections section of the Business Executive Summary. You may use this section for existing businesses as well.

Start-Up Costs	Actual	Budgeted
Accounting Services		
Advertising And Promotion For Opening		
Architectural Design		
Cash		
Decorating		
Utilities		
Equipment, Computers, Furniture, Telephones		
Estimated Taxes		
Headhunting or Other Hiring Costs		
Installation Of Equipment		
Insurance		
Legal Costs (incorporation, filing fees, etc.)		
Licenses And Permits		
Moving		
Office Supplies		
Print Design		
Printing		
Remodeling, Build out		
Rents		
Salaries		
Payroll Taxes & Benefits		
Software		
Starting Inventory		
Unanticipated expenses		
Vehicles		
Website		
Other		
Other		
Other		
Total Start-Up Costs		
Suggested Operating Capital To Break Even		

APPENDIX III
BUSINESS SELECTION WORKSHEET

The following worksheet will help you choose the business that's right for you. It's important that you take the time to seriously evaluate all aspects. To fill it out, follow these three steps:

1. First, list the business ideas you're considering by order of interest. In the top left-hand blank space put the idea you think you're most interested in. Underneath it put the next idea and so forth.

2. Then, take each idea and rate it in each of the areas. Use the following rating system:

   Rating   0 - none
                   1 - below average
                   2 - average
                   3 - above average

3. Finally, total up the numbers. Here are some tips for making sense of the numbers and for narrowing your list of business possibilities:

   ❑ eliminate any of your ideas that scored less than a total of 10

   ❑ eliminate any idea that did not score at least a 2 in every category

   ❑ eliminate any idea that did not score at least a 3 in the uniqueness category

How many ideas are left? If the answer is "none," then you need to use to identify where you need to improve and you need to develop a strategy for raising the "1's" to "2's" or "3's." If the answer is "more than one," you have a pleasant dilemma. If the answer is "one," you may have just found the business that's perfect for you.

YOUR KNOWLEDGE OF THE BUSINESS

How much do you know about the area? Will you have to spend extra time and money teaching yourself the business? Will you have to take on a partner because you don't know the business well enough?

Rating:	0 - No knowledge of the business
		1 - Some indirect knowledge of the business
		2 - Limited knowledge
		3 - Working knowledge

YOUR EXPERIENCE IN THE FIELD

In some cases, you may have a lot of knowledge about the subject, but not much experience. Have you ever worked in this type of business before? To what extent is experience crucial to the business?

Rating:	0 - No experience;
		1 - Indirect experience;
		2 - Limited experience;
		3 - Familiar with the business.

YOUR SKILLS
Ignore, for now, those skills that might be common to each of your ideas, and try to concentrate on skills that are unique to that specific idea. To what extent do you possess those skills? If you lack them, how difficult will it be to acquire them?

Rating:	0 - None;
		1 - Limited skills;
		2 - Some skills;
		3 - Extensive skills.

Business idea	Your knowledge	Your experience	Your skills	Ease of entry	Uniqueness	Total

APPENDIX IV

BUSINESS ANALYSIS WORKSHEET

This worksheet will help you determine how successful you will be if you enter a given business and sell a given product. Assign each business opportunity and product a column number. Answer each question along the left-hand side of the form assigning a rating of 1-3, with 3 being the strongest. Total each column after you've finished. The opportunity and product with the highest total points are your strongest candidates for success.

Business Opportunity	Bus 1	Bus 2	Bus 3	Bus 4
Relevance of your previous experience to opportunity				
Familiarity with daily operations of this type of business				
Compatibility of business with your investment goals				
Compatibility of business with your income goals				
Likely profitability of business				
Likelihood of business to meet your desire for personal fulfillment				
Projected growth for the industry				
Acceptability of risk level				
Acceptability of hours you will need to work				
Column Totals				

Product Marketability	Prod 1	Prod 2	Prod 3	Prod 4
Probability of use by target market				
Compatibility with image desired				
Competitiveness of price				
Number and strength of marketable features				
Probability that product will enhance sales of current line				
Projected stability of demand				
Ability to overcome seasonal or cyclical resistance				
Uniqueness of product				
Ability of business to obtain needed equipment				
Likely acceptance potential				
Ability of business to afford the development and production of product				
Column Totals				
Total Scores				

APPENDIX V

2010 ACCOUNTING SOFTWARE REVIEW PRODUCT COMPARISON TABLE

GO TO:

HTTP://ACCOUNTING-SOFTWARE-REVIEW.TOPTENREVIEWS.COM/

APPENDIX VI

[YOUR COMPANY NAME] BUSINESS PLAN

> Insert a color company logo or picture representing company or product/service

[YOUR NAME]
[YOUR TITLE]
[YOUR ADDRESS]
[YOUR ADDRESS 2]
[YOUR CITY, STATE/PROVINCE, ZIP/POSTAL CODE]
[YOUR PHONE NUMBER]
[YOUR EMAIL@YOURCOMPANY.COM]
[YOUR WEBSITE ADDRESS]
[DATE]

Business Plan
Table of Contents

Statement of Confidentiality & Non-Disclosure

Executive Summary
- Business Description
- Products and Services
- The Market
- Competition
- Operations
- Management Team
- Risks & Opportunities
- Financial Summary
- Capital Requirements

Section I Business Description
    1.1 Industry Overview
    1.2 Company Description
    1.3 History and Current Status
    1.4 Goals and Objectives
    1.5 Critical Success Factors
    1.6 Company Ownership
    1.7 Exit Strategy

Section II   **Products and Services**
    2.1 Description of Products or Services
    2.2 Unique/Proprietary Features of Products or Services
    2.3 Research and Development
    2.4 Production
    2.5 New and Follow-Up Products or Services

Section III   **The Market**
    3.1 Industry Analysis
    3.2 Market Analysis
    3.3 Competitor Analysis

Section IV	**Marketing Strategies and Sales**
    4.1 Introduction
    1.2 Market Segmentation Strategy
    1.3 Targeting Strategy
    1.4 Positioning Strategy
    1.5 Products/Services Strategy
    1.6 Pricing Strategy
    1.7 Distribution Channels
    1.8 Promotion and Advertising Strategy
    1.9 Sales Strategy
    1.10 Sales Forecast

Section V	**Development**
    5.1 Development Strategy
    5.2 Development Timeline
    5.3 Development Expenses

Section VI	**Management**
    6.1 Company Organization
    6.2 Management Team
    6.3 Management Structure and Style
    6.4 Ownership
    6.5 Board of Directors (or Advisors)

Section VII	**Operations**
    7.1 Operations Strategy
    7.2 Scope of Operations
    7.3 Ongoing Operations
    7.4 Location
    7.5 Personnel
    7.6 Production
    7.7 Operations Expenses
    7.8 Legal Environment
    7.9 Inventory
    7.10 Suppliers
    7.11 Credit Policies

Section VIII   **Financials**
8.1 Start-Up Funds
8.2 Financial History and Analysis
8.3 Current Financial Position
8.4 Operating Forecast
8.5 Breakeven Analysis
8.6 Balance Sheet
8.7 Income Statement
8.8 Cash Flow Statement

Section IX   **Offering or Funding Request**
9.1 Offer
9.2 Capital Requirements
9.3 Risks and Opportunities
9.4 Valuation of Business
9.5 Exit Strategy

Section X   **Refining the Plan**
10.1 Raising Capital
10.2 Type of Business

Section XI   **Appendix**

APPENDIX VII

Marketing Plan

Statement of Confidentiality and Non-Disclosure

Executive Summary

Section I Situation Analysis
    1.1 Industry Analysis
    1.2 Sales Analysis
    1.3 Competitive Analysis
    1.4 Customer Analysis
    1.5 S.W.O.T. Analysis
    1.6 Analysis of Marketing Activities

Section II   **Objectives**
    2.1 Corporate Objectives
    2.2 Marketing Objectives

Section III   **Marketing Strategy**
    3.1 Market Segmentation Strategy
    3.2 Targeting Strategy
    3.3 Product Life Cycles
    3.4 Potential Strategies
    3.5 Core Strategy

Section IV   **Marketing Programs**
    4.1 Marketing Mix
    4.2 Loyalty Programs
    4.3 Customer Service & Support
    4.4 Market Research
    4.5 Personal Selling
    4.6 Trust & Credibility
    4.7 Trade Programs

Section V   **Implementation Plan**
                      5.1 Product Design & Development
                      5.2 Sales & Marketing
                      5.3 Distributors
                      5.4 Resource Requirements
                      5.5   Scheduling

Section VI   **Performance Evaluation & Monitoring**
                      6.1 Monitoring Ad Campaigns Sales Analysis
                      6.2 Profit & Loss Statements
                      6.3 Meeting Schedules
                      6.4 Customer Profiling
                      6.5 Sales Force Evaluation

Section VII   **Financial Information**
                      7.1 Financial Capsule
                      7.2 Financial Assumptions
                      7.3 Marketing Budget
                      7.4 Sales Projections (3-5 years)

Section VIII   **Contingency Plans**
                      8.1 Symptoms of Failure
                      8.2 Alternate Strategies

Section IX   **Appendices**

NOTE: *If you have an established business and are looking to expand the complexity and detail of a marketing plan, following is more detail to help define the elements of a plan. If you are a new entrepreneur, it will not be necessary to implement this level of detail. The only exception would be if you are seeking a very large sum of money as a capital investment to get your business started. Investors will have an expectancy that you will have not only a high level of knowledge about these elements but that you know how to implement them, track them and generate a significant return on investment.*

Situation Analysis

Industry Analysis

Market Characteristics

1. Market size (in dollars and/or production units)
2. growth rate (annual rate in percentage) by geographical region
3. Market potential, industry/expert forecasts
4. History of market (how it has evolved), market stage (e.g. new market, mature market, etc.)
5. Level of competition, dominant players, presence of conglomerates, noticeable past failures, noticeable new entries
6. Trends in supply and demand

Trends and Drivers

1. Major industry trends, fashion and fads
2. Major drivers of change
3. Changes in use of product
4. New categories of product users based on demographics such as age, gender, income, education, occupation, etc. or based on psychographics such as benefits desired, habits, values, attitudes, lifestyle, behavior, opinions, etc.
5. Demand cycles, seasonality effect (summer vs. winter), special occasions, and worldwide events

Sales Analysis:
1. Economic growth and profitability of industry vs. your growth and profitability
2. Evolution of sales, market share, variable costs (labor, raw materials, energy, etc.)

Competitive Analysis

Competitive landscape

1. Indicate level of competition in industry (e.g. fierce, moderate) and number of competitors
2. Identify volatility of competition in industry: number of new players and failures each year
3. Describe types of competition affecting your business
4. Identify the industry's competitive barriers to overcome and state how your company will deal with them
5. Identify potential sources of competitive advantage

Key Players

1. Identify major and secondary competitors (direct competitors, indirect competitors, substitutes, potential entrants, related products) and evaluate relative intensity of competition arising from each source

2. Identify the factors that give power to competitors (e.g. marketing strategy, superior product, established company, strong financial backing, expertise, relationship with key industry members, etc.)

3. Identify the strategies and/or market conditions that have allowed competitors to achieve good results and, if applicable, what has caused them to fail

Key Players vs. Your Company

1. Select your main competitors and compare them to your company. Evaluate the performance of their marketing activities and identify the intensity and type of threat they pose, main strategies, recent initiatives and offensive tactics (that may be directed towards your company).

2. Briefly analyze the following elements and compare them to your company:

- Product/service offering (characteristics, features, benefits)
- Size (in terms of sales, market share, infrastructure and customer base)
- Objectives
- Strengths and weaknesses
- Brand equity: customer loyalty, brand image, brand awareness, brand recognition and brand reputation
- Past, present and future strategies
- Marketing strategies (positioning, branding, advertising, media expenditures)
- Probable actions in response to market changes and to your company
- Efficiencies in cost structure (e.g. economies of scale or scope, streamlined processes, JIT, etc.)
- Degree of vertical integration
- History of innovations
- Strength of management
- Strength of distribution
- Financial resources

Customer Analysis

1. Identify expected changes in target customer needs
2. Identify expected changes in buying behavior
3. Identify expected changes in customer perceptions and attitudes and how these changes might affect competitors' strategy
4. Identify segments that might potentially become your target
5. Provide forecasted changes in market segments: Which segments are growing or declining and why?
6. Growth rate
7. Relative segment sizes

S.W.O.T. Analysis

List your company's strengths, weaknesses, opportunities and threats

Objectives
1. Corporate Objectives
2. Marketing Objectives (short term and long term)

Marketing Strategy

Targeting Strategy

The three main targeting strategies are:
1. ***Mass Marketing***: go after the entire market with one offer that addresses common needs
2. ***Differentiated Marketing***: go after several market segments with tailored offers
3. ***Target Marketing***: go after a smaller segment with a tailored offer
   Target Marketing can be done using:

   ### Demographics
   - Age
   - Gender
   - Social status
   - Occupation
   - Religion
   - Ethnicity
   - Income
   - Social class

   ### Psychographics
   - Lifestyle
   - Attitudes and beliefs
   - Perceptions

Usage patterns
- Buying motives
- When, where and how they buy
- Usage rate
- How often they buy
- Types of important buying situations
- Who makes the buying decision and who does the buying?

Marketing and Brand dimensions
- Specific responses to marketing campaigns
- Openness to marketing
- Familiarity with brand
- Do they select a product based on brand or product attributes?
- Brand loyalty
- Customer satisfaction
- How they choose between competing brands

Nature of your relationship with customers
- Face-to-face, telephone, Internet, mail
- Closeness of the relationship
- How often is their feedback requested?
- How often do you communicate with them?

Core Strategy

There are many different kinds of marketing strategies. Select from the list below which one(s) will be employed by your company.

1. Aggressive tactics
2. Defensive marketing
3. Maintain steady growth
4. Guerilla marketing
5. Traditional marketing (print, radio, TV, outdoors, public relations)
6. Grassroots marketing: word of mouth, viral marketing, buzz marketing
7. Interactive marketing, digital marketing

8. Direct marketing, relationship marketing
9. Urban marketing
10. Lifestyle marketing, experiential marketing, events marketing
11. Youth-oriented marketing
12. Loyalty marketing
13. Entire market coverage or selected segments
14. Unique packaging
15. Exclusive/wide distribution

Implementation of Sales & Marketing Plan

Pricing Requirements
1. Detail new pricing structures
2. Costs
3. Wholesale price
4. Markup
5. Suggested retail price

Positioning, Branding & Corporate Literature

1. Determine the company's positioning and brand strategies
2. Determine corporate style guide and creative guidelines for using brands, logos, slogans, company fonts, color scheme, etc.

Advertising

1. Research, plan, create, review, approve and test advertisements and for placing media buys

Financial Information

    Financial Assumptions: List the assumptions you use when creating your financial models

    Marketing Budget: Create a marketing budget. This is different than your company's operating budget. It should include only elements of sales and marketing.

    Sales Projections: Project future sales for the next 3 to 5 years

Glossary of Terms

A

Accounts Payable — Trade accounts of businesses representing obligations to pay for goods and services received.

Accounts Receivable— Trade accounts of businesses representing moneys due for goods sold or services rendered evidenced by notes, statements, invoices, or other written evidence of a present obligation.

Accounting — The recording, classifying, summarizing, and interpreting in a significant manner and in terms of money, transactions, and events of a financial character.

Accredited Investor — An individual who meets one or more of the following: $1 million or more in net worth; income in excess of $200,000 in each of the last two years; or a joint income with a spouse exceeding $300,000 in each of the last two years.

Angel Groups — Organizations, funds and networks (i.e. Colorado Capital Alliance) formed for the specific purpose of facilitating angel investments in start-up companies.

Angel Investors — Sophisticated, accredited investors who choose to make early stage investments in the form of time and money in start-up companies.

Anti-dilution Clause — The means by which one preserves a percentage of ownership in the company without having to make a new investment. One does not have to pay in order to maintain their position.
    Typical — Provides for protection in the event of a stock split, stock dividend or similar recapitalization.
    Full Ratchet — Complete preservation of percentage ownership in all circumstances including protection in the event of a subsequent sale or merger.

Modified Ratchet — Does not provide for "ratcheting" in limited circumstances such as new subsequent offerings at prices lower than per share investment price ("down rounds") or employee equity offerings.

Assumption — The act of assuming or undertaking another's debts or obligations.

Auction — A public sale of goods to the highest bidder.

Automatic Conversion — Under certain circumstances, such as the company going public or a majority of *Series X* shareholders voting to convert, all *Series X* shares will be converted 1:1 into common shares. Sometimes referred to as "forced conversion".

Automatic Data Processing — Data processing largely performed by automatic means. The discipline which deals with methods and techniques of automatic data processing. Pertaining to data processing equipment such as electrical accounting machines and electronic data processing equipment.

B

Bankruptcy — A condition in which a business cannot meet its debt obligations and petitions a federal district court for either reorganization of its debts or liquidation of its assets. In the action the property of a debtor is taken over by a receiver or trustee in bankruptcy for the benefit of the creditors. This action is conducted as prescribed by the National Bankruptcy Act, and may be voluntary or involuntary.

Breakeven Point — The breakeven point in any business is that point at which the volume of sales or revenues exactly equals total expenses - the point at which there is neither a profit nor loss - under varying levels of activity. The breakeven point tells the manager what level of output or activity is required before the firm can make a profit; reflects the relationship between costs, volume, and profits.

Bridge Financing — Interim financing of one sort or another used to solidify a position until more permanent financing is arranged.

Bridge Loan — A short-term loan that is used until a person or company can secure permanent financing. Usually in the form of debt convertible into equity issued during the next round of financing.

Brokers — Private individuals or firms retained by early-stage companies to raise funds for a finder's fee.

Broker Dealer — Any individual or firm in the business of buying and selling securities for itself and others. Broker/dealers must register with the SEC. When acting as a broker, a broker/dealer executes orders on behalf of his/her client. When acting as a dealer, a broker/dealer executes trades for his/her firm's own account. Securities bought for the firm's own account may be sold to clients or other firms, or become a part of the firm's holdings.

Business Birth — Formation of a new establishment or enterprise.

Business Death —Voluntary or involuntary closure of a firm or establishment.

Business Dissolution — For enumeration purposes, the absence from any current record of a business that was present in a prior time period.

Business Failure —The closure of a business causing a loss to at least one creditor.

Business Plan —A comprehensive planning document which clearly describes the business developmental objective of an existing or proposed business applying for assistance in SBA's 8(a) or lending programs. The plan outlines what and how and from where the resources needed to accomplish the objective will be obtained and utilized.

Business Start — For enumeration purposes, a business with a name or similar designation that did not exist in a prior time period.

C

C Corporation — A separate entity, with legal existence apart from its owners, the stockholders.

Call — An option that gives the holder the right to buy the underlying asset. Opposite of a put.

Call Provision — An embedded option granting a bond issuer the right to buy back all or part of an issue prior to maturity.

Canceled Loan — The annulment or rescission of an approved loan prior to disbursement.

Capital — Assets less liabilities, representing the ownership interest in a business; a stock of accumulated goods, especially at a specified time and in contrast to income received during a specified time period; accumulated goods devoted to the production of goods; (4) accumulated possessions calculated to bring income.

Capital Expenditures — Business spending on additional plant equipment and inventory.

Capitalization — The debt and/or equity mix that funds a company's assets.

Capitalization Table (Cap Table) — A table describing the capitalization of a company including the names and number of shares owned by each principal and investors. This table is often segmented to describe each of several funding rounds in the company and clearly differentiates preferred and common shareholders.

Capitalized Property — Personal property of the agency which has an average dollar value of $300.00 or more and a life expectancy of one year or more. Capitalized property shall be depreciated annually over the expected useful life to the agency.

Cash Discount — An incentive offered by the seller to encourage the buyer to pay within a stipulated time. For example, if the terms are 2/10/N 30, the buyer may deduct 2 percent from the amount of the invoice (if paid within 10 days); otherwise, the full amount is due in 30 days.

Cash Flow — An accounting presentation showing how much of the cash generated by the business remains after both expenses (including interest) and principal repayment on financing are paid. A projected cash flow statement indicates whether the business will have cash to pay its expenses, loans, and make a profit. Cash flows can be calculated for any given period of time, normally done on a monthly basis.

Character — A letter, digit, or other symbol that is a part of the organization, control, or representation of data used in computer systems.

Charge-off — An accounting transaction removing an uncollectible balance from the active receivable accounts.

Charged-off Loan — An uncollectible loan for which the principal and accrued interest were removed from the receivable accounts.

Closing — Actions and procedures required to affect the documentation and disbursement of loan funds after the application has been approved and the execution of all required documentation and its filing and recording where required.

Closed Loan — Any loan for which funds have been disbursed and all required documentation has been executed, received, and reviewed. For statistical purposes, first or total disbursement is counted as a closed loan.

Collateral — Something of value - securities, evidence of deposit, or other property - pledged to support the repayment of an obligation.

Collateral Document — A legal document covering the item(s) pledged as collateral on a loan, i.e., note, mortgages, assignment, etc.

Common Stock — Securities that represent equity ownership in a company. Common shares let an investor vote on such matters as the election of directors. They also give the holder a share in a company's profits via dividend payments or the capital appreciation of the security. Units of ownership of a public corporation with junior status to the claims of secured/unsecured creditors, bondholders and preferred shareholders in the event of liquidation. Founders and employees almost always own shares or options for common stock.

Compromise — The settlement of a claim resulting from a defaulted loan for less than the full amount due. Compromise settlement is a procedure available for use only in instances where the government cannot collect the full amount due within a reasonable time, by enforced collection proceedings, or where the cost of such proceedings would not justify such effort.

Consortium — A coalition of organizations, such as banks and corporations, set up to fund ventures requiring large capital resources.

Contingent Liability — A potential obligation that may be incurred dependent upon the occurrence of a future event. Two examples are: (1) the liability of an endorser or guarantor of a note if the primary borrower fails to pay as agreed and (2) the liability that would be incurred if a pending lawsuit is resolved in the other party's favor.

Conversion Rights — Rights by which preferred stock "converts" into common stock. Usually, one has this right at any time after making an investment. Company may want rights to force a conversion upon an IPO, upon hitting of certain sales or earnings' targets, or upon a majority or supermajority vote of the preferred stock. Conversion rights may carry with them anti-dilution protections.

Convertible Preferred Stock — Most common security for venture capital investments. Holders of this class of stock have "preference" over the common shareholders in the event of a liquidation of the company. Preferred shareholders can receive dividends, exercise voting privileges and retain the option to convert to common stock.

Corporation — A group of persons granted a state charter legally recognizing them as a separate entity having its own rights, privileges, and liabilities distinct from those of its members. The process of incorporating should be completed with the state's secretary of state or state corporate counsel, and usually requires the services of an attorney.

Co-Sale Provisions or Rights — Allows investors to sell their shares of stock in the same proportions and for the same terms as the founders, managers, or other investors, should any of those parties receive an offer.

Costs — Money obligated for goods and services received during a given period of time, regardless of when ordered or whether paid for.

Credit Rating — A grade assigned to a business concern to denote the net worth and credit standing to which the concern is entitled in the opinion of the rating agency as a result of its investigation.

Cumulative Voting — A system of voting for directors of a corporation in which shareholder's total number of votes is equal to the number of shares held times the number of candidates.

D

Data Element — The basic unit of identifiable and definable information. A data element occupies the space provided by fields in a record or blocks on a form. It has an identifying name and value or values for expressing a specific fact. For example, a data element named "Color of Eyes" could have recorded values of "Blue (a name)," "Bl (an abbreviation)," "06 (a code)." Similarly, a data element named "Age of Employee" could have a recorded value of "28" (a numeric value).

Deal Structure – An agreement made between the investor and the company defining the rights and obligations of the parties involved. The process by which one arrives at the final terms and conditions of the investment.

Debenture — Debt instrument evidencing the holder's right to receive interest and principal installments from the named obligor. Applies to all forms of unsecured, long-term debt evidenced by a certificate of debt.

Debt Capital — Business financing that normally requires periodic interest payments and repayment of the principal within a specified time.

Debt Financing — The provision of long term loans to a business concern in exchange for debt securities or a note.

Deed of Trust — A document under seal which, when delivered, transfers a present interest in property. May be held as collateral.

Default — The nonpayment of principal and/or interest on the due date as provided by the terms and conditions of the note.

Deferred Loan — Loans whose principal and or interest installments are postponed for a specified period of time.

Demand Registration Rights — A negotiated right of investors to convert private ownership in the company through registration as shares eligible for trading in public markets.

Dilution — The reduction in percentage ownership of the company that investors experience due to subsequent funding rounds.

Disbursement — The actual payout to borrower of loan funds, in whole or part. It may be concurrent with the closing or follow it.

Disbursing Officer — An employee authorized to pay out cash or issue checks in settlement of vouchers approved by a certifying officer.

Divestiture — Change of ownership and/or control of a business from a majority (non-disadvantaged) to disadvantaged persons.

Dividends — Proceeds paid by the company as a return on an original investment. Generally, they are discretionary with the company and aren't paid unless contracted for or after the company has gone public. Dividends can be paid either in cash or in kind, i.e. additional shares of stock.
    Cumulative — Missed dividend payments that continue to accrue.
    Non-cumulative — Missed dividend payments that do not accrue.
    Participating — Dividends which share (participate) with common stock.
    Non-participating — Dividends which do not share with common stock.

Down Round — Price per share is less than in the previous round of financing. (See *Turnaround Financing*)

Due Diligence — Process of validating a potential investment. Usually involves the study of six areas of a company's business plan: market structure, competition and strategy; technology assessment; management team; operating plan; financial review; and legal review. Checking the references of the principals is a critical portion of this process.

E

Earning Power — The demonstrated ability of a business to earn a profit, over time, while following good accounting practices. When a business shows a reasonable profit on invested capital after fully maintaining the business property, appropriately compensating its owner and employees, servicing its obligations, and fully recognizing its costs, the business may be said to have demonstrated earning power. Demonstrated earning power is the foremost test of the business risk in pressing upon an application for a loan.

Easement — A right or privilege that a person may have on another's land, as the right of a way or ingress or egress.

Employee Assistance Program (EAP) Coordinator — Coordinates the activities of Central Office or regional counselors, maintains a community resource list of available professional assistance to troubled employees, and a current roster of EAP counselors for the area of his/her jurisdiction.

EAP Counselor — Conducts confidential consultations with troubled employees who so request, who are referred for objective analysis of a personal problem, and for identification of the best available assistance and/or professional services needed to resolve the employee's problem.

Enterprise — Aggregation of all establishments owned by a parent company. An enterprise can consist of a single, independent establishment or it can include subsidiaries or other branch establishments under the same ownership and control.

Entrepreneur — One who assumes the financial risk of the initiation, operation, and management of a given business or undertaking.

Equity — An ownership interest in a business.

Equity Financing — The provision of funds for capital or operating expenses in exchange for capital stock, stock purchase warrants, and options in the business financed without any guaranteed return, but with the opportunity to share in the company's profits. Equity financing includes long-term subordinated securities containing stock options and/or warrants. Utilized in SBIC financing activities.

Equity Partnership — A limited partnership arrangement for providing startup and seed capital to businesses.

Escrow — Funds placed in trust with a third party by a borrower for a specific purpose and to be delivered to the borrower only upon the fulfillment of certain conditions.

Establishment — A single-location business unit, which may be independent - called a single- establishment enterprise - or owned by a parent enterprise.

Equity — Ownership interest in a company, usually in the form of stock or stock options.

Exit Strategy (aka Liquidity Event) — A planned action taken by a company that results in liquidation of the company's stock, often in the form of an acquisition by a publicly traded company or an IPO.

F

Financial Reports — Reports commonly required from applicants request for financial assistance, e.g.:

Balance Sheet - A report of the status of a firm's assets, liabilities and owner's equity at a given time.

Income Statement - A report of revenue and expense which shows the results of business operations or net income for a specified period of time.

Financing — New funds provided to a business, by either loans, purchase of debt securities, or capital stock.

Finder — Someone who acts as an intermediary for a client in a transaction.

Finder's Fee — A fee paid to someone who acts as an intermediary for a client in a transaction.

Fair Market Value (FMV) — An acceptable selling price to an independent third party.

First Close — An early close of part of a round of financing upon the agreement of all parties.

First Refusal Rights — A negotiated obligation of the company or existing investors to offer shares to the company or other existing investors at fair market value or a previously negotiated price, prior to selling shares to new investors.

Flow Chart — A graphical representation for the definition, analysis, or solution of a problem, in which symbols are used to represent operations, data, flow, equipment, etc.

Foreclosure — The act by the mortgagee or trustee upon default in the payment of interest or principal of a mortgage of enforcing payment of the debt by selling the underlying security.

Forced Buyback — Redemption of convertible debt, convertible preferred stock or common stock on pre-specified terms in situations where the company's value has not appreciated according to the agreed upon plan.

Franchising — A continuing relationship in which the franchisor provides a licensed privilege to the franchisee to do business and offers assistance in organizing, training, merchandising, marketing, and managing in return for a consideration. Franchising is a form of business by which the owner (franchisor) of a product, service, or method obtains distribution through affiliated dealers (franchisees). The product, method, or service being marketed is usually identified by the franchisor's brand name, and the holder of the privilege (franchisee) is often given exclusive access to a defined geographical area.

G

Gross Domestic Product (GDP) — The most comprehensive single measure of aggregate economic output. Represents the market value of the total output of the goods and services produced by a nation's economy.

Gross National Product (GNP) — A measure of a nation's aggregate economic output. Since 1991 GDP, a slightly different calculation, has replaced GNP as a measure of U.S. economic output.

Guaranteed Loan — A loan made and serviced by a lending institution under agreement that a governmental agency will purchase the guaranteed portion if the borrower defaults.

H

Hardware — A term used to describe the mechanical, electrical, and electronic elements of a data processing system.

Harvest — Reaping the benefits of investment in a privately held company by selling the company for cash or stock in a publicly held company, also to execute the exit strategy.

Hazard Insurance — Insurance required showing lender as loss payee covering certain risks on real and personal property used for securing loans.

I

Incubator — A facility designed to encourage entrepreneurship and minimize obstacles to new business formation and growth, particularly for high technology firms, by housing a number of fledgling enterprises that share an array of services. These shared services may include meeting areas, secretarial services, accounting services, research libraries, on-site financial and management counseling, and word processing facilities.

Independent and Qualified Public Accountants — Public accountants are independent when neither they nor any of their family have a material, direct, or indirect financial interest in the borrower other than as an accountant. They are qualified, unless there is contrary evidence, when they are either (1) certified, licensed, or otherwise registered if so required by the state in which they work, or (2) have worked as a public accountant for at least five years and are accepted by SBA.

Industrial Revenue Bond (IRB) — A tax-exempt bond issued by a state or local government agency to finance industrial or commercial projects that serve a public good. The bond usually is not backed by the full faith and credit of the government that issues it, but is repaid solely from the revenues of the project and requires a private sector commitment for repayment.

Information Rights — Rights granting access to company's information, i.e. inspecting the company books and receiving financial statements, budgets and executive summaries.

Innovation — Introduction of a new idea into the marketplace in the form of a new product or service or an improvement in organization or process.

Insolvency — The inability of a borrower to meet financial obligations as they mature or having insufficient assets to pay legal debts.

Intellectual Property (IP) — Right or non-physical resource that is presumed to represent an advantage to a company's position in the marketplace, including patents, trademarks, copyrights and licenses.

Interest — An amount paid a lender for the use of funds.

Intermediary (aka Financial Intermediary) — An individual or institution empowered to make investment decisions for other persons or entities.

IPO (Initial Public Offering) — The regulated process by which a private corporation registers its shares for trading in public markets. Also referred to as "going public".

Inverse Order of Maturity — When payments are received from borrowers that are larger than the authorized repayment schedules, the overpayment is credited to the final installments of the principal, which reduces the maturity of the loan and does not affect the original repayment schedule.

Investment Bankers — Representatives of financial institutions engaged in the issue of new securities, including management and underwriting of issues as well as securities trading and distribution. Licensed by the National Association of Securities Dealers (NASD).

Investment Banking — Businesses specializing in the formation of capital. This is done by outright purchase and sale of securities offered by the issuer, standby underwriting, or "best efforts selling."

Invitation for Bids — Formal solicitations for offerings to perform procurements by competitive bids when the specifications describe the requirements of the government clearly, accurately, and completely, but avoiding unnecessarily restrictive specifications or requirements which might unduly limit the number of bidders.

J

Job Description — A written statement listing the elements of a particular job or occupation, e.g., purpose, duties, equipment used, qualifications, training, physical and mental demands, working conditions, etc.

Judgment — Judicial determination of the existence of an indebtedness or other legal liability.

Judgment by Confession — The act of debtors permitting judgment to be entered against them for a given sum with a statement to that effect, without the institution of legal proceedings.

Junk Bond — A high-yield corporate bond issue with a below-investment rating that became a growing source of corporate funding in the 1980s.

L

LLC (Limited Liability Company) — A legal entity owned by "members" who either manage the business themselves or appoint "managers" to run it for them. All members and managers have the benefit of limited liability, and, in most cases, are taxed in the same way as a subchapter S Corporation without having to conform to the S Corporation restrictions.

Lead investor — Leader among the investors in a round of equity investment in a privately held company, usually also the leader of the due diligence efforts related to the same investment round.

Lease — A contract between the owner (lessor) and the tenant (lessee) stating the conditions under which the tenant may occupy or use the property.

Legal Rate of Interest — The maximum rate of interest fixed by the laws of the various states which a lender may charge a borrower for the use of money.

Lending Institution — Any institution, including a commercial bank, savings and loan association, commercial finance company, or other lender qualified to participate with SBA in the making of loans.

Leveraged Buyout — Takeover of a company, using borrowed funds. Most often, the target company assets serve as security for the loans taken out by the acquiring firm, which repays the loan out of the cash flow of the acquired company.

Lien — A charge upon or security interest in real or personal property maintained to ensure the satisfaction of a debt or duty ordinarily arising by operation of law.

Liquidation — The disposal, at maximum prices, of the collateral securing a loan and the voluntary and enforced collection of the remaining loan balance from the obligators and/or guarantors.

Liquidation Preference — A preference offered to certain investors over the founders and investors in earlier rounds, upon liquidation of the ownership of the company.

Liquidation Value — The net value realizable in the sale (ordinarily a forced sale) of a business or a particular asset.

Litigation — Refers to a loan in "liquidation status" which has been referred to attorneys for legal action.

Also: The practice of taking legal action through the judicial process.

Loan Agreement — Agreement to be executed by borrower, containing pertinent terms, conditions, covenants, and restrictions.

Loan Payoff Amount — The total amount of money needed to meet a borrower's obligation on a loan. It is arrived at by accruing gross interest for one day and multiplying this figure by the number of days that exist between the date of the last repayment and the date on which the loan is to be completely paid off. This amount, known as accrued interest, is combined with the latest principal and escrow balances that are applicable to what is now referred to as the loan payoff amount. In the case where prepaid interest exceeds the accrued interest, the latter is subtracted from the former and the difference is used to reduce the total amount owed.

Lock-up Agreement — Agreements entered into between the lead underwriter and significant stockholders, whereby the stockholders agree not to sell any company stock for a number of predetermined days (usually 180). This time period allows the market to absorb the company's offerings.

Long-form Demand Registration — (*See Registration Rights*)

Loss Rate — A rate developed by comparing the ratio of total loans charged off to the total loans disbursed from inception of the program to the present date.

Loss reserve Adjustment Rate — A reserve rate based upon the ratio of the aggregate net charge-offs (charge-offs less recoveries) for the most recent five years to the total average loans outstanding for the comparable 5-year period.

M

Market Standoff Agreement — Similar to Lock-Up Agreements and prevents selling company stock for a number of predetermined days after a previous stock offering by the company. Typically an IPO.

Mark-up — Markup is the difference between invoice cost and selling price. It may be expressed either as a percentage of the selling price or the cost price and is supposed to cover all the costs of doing business plus a profit. Whether markup is based on the selling price or the cost price, the base is always equal to 100 percent.

Maturity — As applied to securities and commercial paper, the period end date when payment of principal is due.

Maturity Extensions — Extensions of payment beyond the original period established for repayment of a loan.

Merger — A combination of two or more corporations wherein the dominant unit absorbs the passive ones, the former continuing operation usually under the same name. In a consolidation two units combine and are succeeded by a new corporation, usually with a new title.

Mezzanine Financing — Provides funds for further business expansion for companies with a year or two of profitability or an initial public offering.

Mortgage — An instrument giving legal title to secure the repayment of a loan made by the mortgagee (lender). In legal contemplation there are two types: (1) title theory - operates as a transfer of the legal title of the property to the mortgagee, and (2) lien theory - creates a lien upon the property in favor of the mortgagee.

N

Negotiation — The face to face process used by local unions and the employer to exchange their views on those matters involving personnel policies and practices or other matters affecting the working conditions of employees in the unit and reduced to a written binding agreement. Used also by contracting officers to reach agreement with potential contractors.

Negotiation Dispute — That point in negotiations where labor and management cannot come to an agreement on some or all of the issues on the bargaining table and the services of the FMCS have not been utilized.

Negotiated Grievance Procedure — The sole and exclusive procedure available to all employees in a bargaining unit and the employer for processing grievances and disputes.

Net Worth — Property owned (assets), minus debts and obligations owed (liabilities), is the owner's equity (net worth).

Non-Disclosure Agreement (NDA) An agreement which precludes disclosure to third parties of private information revealed by one party to another, usually for a fixed term.

Notes and Accounts Receivable — A secured or unsecured receivable evidenced by a note or open account arising from activities involving liquidation and disposal of loan collateral.

O

Obligations — Technically defined as "amount of orders placed, contracts awarded, services received, and similar transactions during a given period which will require payments during the same or a future period."

Ordinary Interest — Simple interest based on a year of 360 days, contrasting with exact interest having a base year of 365 days.

Over-Subscription — Underwriting term describing a new stock issue for which there are more buyers than available shares.

Outlays — Net disbursements (cash payments in excess of cash receipts) for administrative expenses and for loans and related costs and expenses (e.g., gross disbursements for loans and expenses minus loan repayments, interest and fee income collected, and reimbursements received for services performed for other agencies).

P

Partnership — A legal relationship existing between two or more persons contractually associated as joint principals in a business.

Patent — A patent for an invention is the grant of a property right to the inventor, issued by the Patent and Trademark Office. The term of a new patent is 20 years from the date on which the application for the patent was filed in the United States or, in special cases, from the date an earlier related application was filed, subject to the payment of maintenance fees. US patent grants are effective only within the US, US territories, and US possessions.

Piggyback Registrations Rights — Provides investors and/or company founder(s) the right to sell stock at the IPO (rarely) or a later public offering (more commonly) by adding their shares to the aggregate listed in the registration statement. (*See Registration Rights*)

Post-money Valuation — A company's valuation just after its latest round of funding, equal to the number of shares outstanding times the share price from the latest financing.

Pre-emptive Rights — Each holder of at least "x"% of the common equity of the company (on an as-converted to Common Stock basis) shall have the right to provide financing to the company on the same terms offered to third parties in the amount necessary to maintain such holders pro-rata ownership percentage in the company.

Pre-money Valuation — Valuation of a company agreed-upon by the existing owners and the new investors, immediately prior to a new round of funding.

Preferred Stock — Most likely security for angel investments, it is senior to common stock and junior to debt. Preferred stock is a contract right, i.e. its terms must be set forth clearly in writing in order to obtain the anticipated rights. It can have a variety of voting, dividend, management, conversion and other rights and must be carefully crafted to ensure the upside and protect against the downside.

Prime Rate — Interest rate which is charged to business borrowers having the highest credit ratings for short term borrowing.

Private Placement — The sale of stocks, bonds or other investments directly to institutional or accredited investors. A private placement does not have to be registered with the SEC, as a public offering does, if the securities are purchased for investment as opposed to resale.

Private Placement Memorandum (PPM) — A formal description of an investment opportunity written to comply with various federal securities regulations. A properly prepared PPM is designed to provide specific information to the buyers in order to protect sellers from liabilities related to selling unregistered securities. Typically PPMs contain: a complete description of the security offered for sale, the terms of the sales, and fees; capital structure and historical financial statements; a description of the business; summary biographies of the management team; and the numerous risk factors associated with the investment. In practice, the PPM is not generally used in angel or venture capital deals, since most sophisticated investors perform thorough due diligence on their own and do not rely on the summary information provided by a typical PPM.

Proof of Concept — Product has been proven to work through analysis of the science.

Pro-Net — An Internet-based database of information of small, disadvantaged, 8(a), and women-owned businesses seeking procurement contracts.

Product Liability — Type of tort or civil liability that applies to product manufacturers and sellers.

Professional and Trade Associations — Non-profit, cooperative, and voluntary organizations that are designed to help their members in dealing with problems of mutual interest. In many instances, professional and trade associations enter into an agreement with the SBA to provide volunteer counseling to the small business community.

Proprietorship — The most common legal form of business ownership; about 85 percent of all small businesses are proprietorships. The liability of the owner is unlimited in this form of ownership.

Protest — A statement in writing by any bidder or offeror on a particular procurement alleging that another bidder or offeror on such procurement is not a small business concern.

Public Offering — An offering of new shares of a company made available to the public for purchase. The company must first register its stock with the Securities and Exchange Commission (SEC).

Put — An option granting the right to sell the underlying futures contract. Opposite of a call.

Put Option — An option contract that gives the holder the right to sell a certain quantity of an underlying security to the writer of the option, at a specified price (strike price) up to a specified date (expiration date).

R

Ratchet — Ratchets reduce the price at which venture capitalists can convert their debt into preferred stock, which effectively increases their percentage of equity. Often referred to as an "anti-dilution adjustment."

Ratio — Denotes relationships of items within and between financial statements, e.g., current ratio, quick ratio, inventory turnover ratio, and debt/net worth ratios.

Redemption — Commencing on a predetermined date after the First Close, at the request of the holders of a predetermined percentage of the then outstanding Series X Preferred, the company will redeem the then outstanding Series X Preferred at a redemption price equal to the purchase price plus any accrued and unpaid dividends. Sometimes referred to as a "forced buy-back".

Redemption Rights — Rights to force the company to purchase shares (a "put") and more infrequently the company's right to force investor to sell their shares (a "call"). A Put allows one to liquidate an investment in the event an IPO or public merger becomes unlikely. One may also negotiate a Put effective when the company defaults or fails to make payments upon a key employee's death, etc.

Registration — The process by which a company is authorized by the Securities and Exchange Commission (SEC) to offer shares for sale to the public. Generally involves the disclosure of substantial information on the operations and plans of the company.

Registration Rights — Provisions in the investment agreement that allow investors to sell stock via the public market. Means by which one can transfer shares in compliance with the securities laws subject to Lock-Up and Market Stand-off Agreements.
> *Long-form Demand* — Demand registration before the company becomes public. Usually starts between one to three years after making an investment and may involve one or two demands for a percentage of stock. Company will use the SEC's long-form S-l.
> *Short-form Demand* — Demand made after the company is publicly traded and is eligible to use SEC's Form S-3.
> *Piggyback* — Company is registering stock either for itself or other stockholders and one can "piggyback" a portion of shares for registration onto the company's registration. Usually have these rights for up to five years after the company becomes public, but cannot exercise them for mergers or employee offerings.

Regulation D (Reg D) — An SEC regulation, under the Securities Act of 1933, exempting some private companies, under certain conditions, from the registration requirements of the Act. Provides three different small offering exemptions from registration according to limitations on size of the offering or the number of investors. *Includes rules 504, 505 and 506.*

Rule 504 — Company can raise up to $1 million in any 12-month period from any number of investors provided that the company does not advertise the sale. (See *25102.1(c)*) There are restrictions on the resale of the securities, but there is no requirement of disclosure. Investors need not be sophisticated nor is any formal private offering memorandum required. However, offering is subject to the general antifraud provisions of the federal securities laws requiring that all material information be accurately presented to purchasers.

Rule 505 — Company can raise up to $5 million in a 12-month period. Security sales can be made to an unlimited number of accredited investors plus 35 additional non-accredited investors. Disclosure documents, i.e. a private placement memorandum, must be delivered to all non-accredited investors. If dealing with accredited investors, the number of these is unlimited, but there is no advertising allowed.

Rule 506 — Puts no limit on the amount of money that can be raised, except it must be more than $5 million. No more than 35 non-accredited investors can be involved, and all must be sophisticated. Sellers are restricted from general solicitation and advertising of the sale.

Request for Proposal (RFP) — Solicitations for offerings for competitive negotiated procurements when it is impossible to draft an invitation for bids containing adequate detailed description of the required property and services. There are 15 circumstances in the Federal Acquisition Regulations (FAR) which permit negotiated procurements.

Return on Investment (ROI) — The amount of profit (return) based on the amount of resources (funds) used to produce it. Also, the ability of a given investment to earn a return for its use.

Rights of First Refusal — Right that gives an individual the option of future participation. In private equity, this may be granted to first round investors to participate in future rounds of company financing.

Rule 504 — (See *Regulation D*)

Rule 505 — (See *Regulation D*)

Rule 506 — (See *Regulation D*)

S

S-Corporation — Small business corporation in which the owners personally pay the corporation's income taxes.

Screening Deals — The process used to rate or grade the opportunity presented by new ventures, which is followed by a "go/no-go" decision. Deals that pass the screen receive additional attention by the investors. Those that do not pass the screen are rejected.

Scrubbing Deals — The process of doing "due diligence" on new venture opportunities, prior to making an investment decision.

Secondary Market — Those who purchase an interest in a loan from an original lender, such as banks, institutional investors, insurance companies, credit unions, and pension funds.

Second-stage Financing — Provides capital for expansion. Companies are typically generating revenue and have a sound management team in place, but may not show bottom-line profits.

Seed Financing (aka Seed Capital) — Relatively small amount of financing to an inventor or entrepreneur to prove a concept.

> **Series A** — first round of investment
> **Series B** — second round of investment
> **Series C** — third round of investment

Service Corps of Retired Executives (SCORE) — Retired and working successful business persons who volunteer to render assistance in counseling, training, and guiding small business clients.

Short-form Demand Registration — (*See Registration Rights*)

Sophisticated Investor — An investor with the education, business background and investment experience to be able to obtain the information needed to make reasonable investment decisions about the company in question.

Small Business Development Centers (SBDC) — The SBDC is a university-based center for the delivery of joint government, academic, and private sector services for the benefit of small business and the national welfare. It is committed to the development and productivity of business and the economy in specific geographical regions.

Start-up Financing — Provided to companies completing product development and for early marketing. Companies may be in the process of organizing or may already be in business, but usually have not sold their product commercially.

Stock Option — Grants the right to purchase securities (usually common stock) at a stated exercise price over some future period of time.

Subordinated Debt (aka Junior Debt) — Debt that is either unsecured or has a lower priority than that of another debt claim on the same asset or property.

T

Take Away Provisions — Agreement made between an investor and the management of a company that entitles the investor to penalize the management if the company does not achieve pre-determined results.

Target Multiples — The desired return on investment of private investors in early stage companies, defined in a multiple of the original investment.

Term Sheet — Document that guides lawyers in preparing the investment agreements. Should include at least: agreed-upon valuation of the business including the proposed capitalization table; key financial and legal terms; rights of both parties; and legal obligations of all involved.

Tranche — Funds flowing from investors to a company that represent a partial round or an "early close." Subsequent funds of the single round are generally under the same terms and conditions as the first tranche (or early close); however, those funding the early tranches may receive bonus warrant coverage, in consideration of the additional risk.

Turnaround Financing — Provided to companies, which still show promise, although they have gone through or are currently in a problem period. Often referred to as "Down Round," since investors supplying the turnaround funds will negotiate a stock price lower than that paid by earlier investors. (See *Down Round*)

Turnover (Business) — Turnover is the number of times that an average inventory of goods is sold during a fiscal year or some designated period. Care must be taken to ensure that the average inventory and net sales are both reduced to the same denominator; that is, divide inventory at cost into sales at cost or divide inventory at selling price into sales at selling price. Do not mix cost price with selling price. The turnover, when accurately computed, is one measure of the efficiency of a business.

Turnover (Human Resources) — Turnover is the number of times that the total number of employees is reduced and replaced, for example, if a company begins the year with 100 employees, then during the course of the year the company has 25 employees exit due to terminations or resignations, and those positions are replaced, the Turnover Rate would be 25%.

U

Undelivered Orders — The amount of orders for goods and services outstanding for which the liability has not yet accrued. For practical purposes, represents obligations incurred for which goods have not been delivered or services not performed.

Unfair Labor Practice — Action by either the employer or union which violates the provisions of EO 11491 as amended.

Uniform Commercial Code (UCC) — Codification of uniform laws concerning commercial transactions. In SBA parlance, generally refers to a uniform method of recording and enforcing a security interest or charge upon existing or to be acquired personal property.

Usury — Interest which exceeds the legal rate charged to a borrower for the use of money.

V

Venture Capital — Money used to support new or unusual commercial undertakings; equity, risk, or speculative capital. This funding is provided to new or existing firms that exhibit above-average growth rates, a significant potential for market expansion, and the need for additional financing for business maintenance or expansion.

Venture Capitalist — A financial institution specializing in the provision of equity and other forms of long-term capital to enterprises, usually to firms with a limited track record but with the expectation of substantial growth. The venture capitalist may provide both funding and varying degrees of managerial and technical expertise.

Vesting Schedule — Used in stock options to describe the number of shares that the option recipient can purchase at a defined price and at given dates in the future. Also defines the expiration of said options.

Voluntary Conversion — The optional rights of Series A Preferred shareholders to convert shares of Series X Preferred into shares of common stock of the company at the then applicable conversion ratio, which initially may be one-to-one (Initial Conversion Ratio) and subsequently subject to adjustment.

Voting Rights — A shareholder's rights to vote for the board of directors and other important events such as sales and mergers. Sometimes divided upon the following lines:
    Full — Vote with common stock on each matter as if the preferred shares had been converted into common shares.
    Class — Corporate statute or certificate of incorporation provide a class vote allowing certain preferred stock to vote separately on matters such as sales or mergers. It may be that a particular class of preferred stock votes alone or that all classes of preferred stock vote together.
    Right to Elect Director(s) — Guaranteed right to elect one or more directors to the board.
    Special — Vetoes over certain matters voting. More common in venture investments.

W

Warrants — Securities that give holders the right, but not the obligation, to buy shares of common stock at a fixed price for a given period of time. Similar to stock options (for non-employees) and often offered to investors as a bonus for cash investment or to service providers in exchange for fees.

Word Processing —The efficient and effective production of written communications at the lowest possible cost through the combined use of systems management procedures, automated technology, and accomplished personnel. The equipment used in word processing applications includes but is not limited to the following: dictation and transcription equipment, automatic repetitive typewriters, visual display text editing typewriters, keyboard terminals, etc.

Workers' Compensation — A state-mandated form of insurance covering workers injured in job-related accidents. In some states the state is the insurer; in other states insurance must be acquired from commercial insurance firms. Insurance rates are based on a number of factors, including salaries, firm history, and risk of occupation.

Z
Zero-based Budget — A budget that has a net operating profit of zero; showing no profit or loss.

www.ingramcontent.com/pod-product-compliance
Lightning Source LLC
Chambersburg PA
CBHW031838170526
45157CB00001B/344